THE TIMES

ON

THIS

DAY

Published by Times Books
An imprint of HarperCollins Publishers
Westerhill Road
Bishopbriggs
Glasgow G64 2QT

www.harpercollins.co.uk
times.books@harpercollins.co.uk

First edition 2018

A catalogue record for this book is available from the British Library.

ISBN 978-0-00-831362-3

10 9 8 7 6 5 4 3 2

Printed and bound in Great Britain by CPI Group (UK) Ltd.,
Croydon, CR0 4YY

Cover image © ShabbyPie / Shutterstock

My thanks and acknowledgements go to Lily Cox and Robin
Ashton at News Syndication and, in particular, at The Times,
Ian Brunskill and, at HarperCollins, Gerry Breslin, Jethro Lennox,
Karen Midgley, Kerry Ferguson, Sarah Woods and Evelyn Sword.

INTRODUCTION

In amongst the unchanging, comforting bric-a-brac of the Register section of each edition of *The Times* nestles the record of anniversaries of events which fall "On This Day". The feature has the feel of having been there for ever, alongside the royal engagements and what the weather has in store. Yet in fact, in terms of the newspaper's two centuries and more of history, it is a relatively recent innovation, with this selection compiled from those entries which have appeared during the last decade or so.

They are not meant to represent a complete history of the world. Rather, they are a random, often quirky, frequently diverting list of things you feel better for knowing. That said, the collective mind that put them together seems to have had some idiosyncratic interests, including notable firsts in astronomy, key moments in Britain's withdrawal from empire, and opera premieres. The broad-minded reader of *The Times* naturally takes all these in his or her stride. What can the rest of us learn from this midden heap of the past?

Perhaps it is that the past is just that. Rooting about in it disinters things which were once prized but are now of little account. Events which made headlines – "40 skaters drowned in Regent's Park" – are long forgotten. How quickly things change, one might think (maybe contemplating an entry whilst adding to one's own midden heap), a thought soon followed by: "Did that happen 20 years ago already?"

And then there are the secret harmonies one fancies hearing in time's dance music. Can it be just coincidence that Sir Winston Churchill died on the same day of the year (January 24th) as not only his father but also Sir John Vanbrugh, architect of the Churchills' family seat at Blenheim? That Rolls-Royce should commission its proud emblem *Spirit of Ecstasy* exactly 60 years to the day before declaring bankruptcy? What unseen force sent King Louis XVI to the guillotine on the anniversary of its inventor having proposed it as a humane method of execution?

Another newspaper – now itself passed into history – once claimed of its contents that "All human life is here". That may not be precisely true of this selection, but it is good to be reminded of the breadth and diversity of mankind's achievements. Sometimes one can even be surprised by them: Mary Shelley wrote *Frankenstein* when she was 21; Sid Vicious rose to fame with the Sex Pistols when a year younger; the first public flushing lavatory for women opened in London as early as 1852.

So, read on and find your own path through the past, be it by lucky dip, joining the dots, using the date index at the back of the book or through dates that mean something to you. Discover something that prompts you to learn more, or to think "I never knew that!", a fact to share with a friend and make you muse upon all that has gone before us down the ages: a glorious gallimaufry of happenings.

And then turn the page and read the Obituaries.

James Owen

ON THIS DAY

1 JANUARY

1785 *The Daily Universal Register* was founded. It was renamed *The Times* on January 1, 1788.

·

1801 the Acts of Union between Great Britain and Ireland came into force.

·

1901 the Commonwealth of Australia was established, allowing the nation to govern itself.

·

1962 the Beatles were not signed by Decca Records because guitar groups were "on the way out".

·

1973 Britain entered the Common Market, later named the European Union.

·

1999 the euro was introduced, giving 11 countries a shared currency — the first time since the Roman Empire that much of Europe had had one.

2 JANUARY

17 Roman poet Ovid died, a decade after mysteriously being banished to modern-day Romania by Emperor Augustus.

•

1769 the Royal Academy met for the first time, with Sir Joshua Reynolds as president.

•

1896 Leander Starr Jameson surrendered after his raid failed to provoke an uprising by British workers against the Boers in the Transvaal.

•

1959 the Russians launched the rocket Luna 1 on the first close fly-by mission to the moon.

•

1971 66 football fans were killed in a crush at Ibrox Park, Glasgow.

•

1981 police arrested serial killer Peter Sutcliffe, the Yorkshire Ripper.

1521 the Pope excommunicated Martin Luther, founder of Protestantism.

•

1892 JRR Tolkein, author of *The Hobbit* and *The Lord of the Rings*, was born.

•

1924 Howard Carter discovered the sarcophagus of Tutankhamun in the Valley of the Kings, Egypt.

•

1946 William Joyce (better known as Lord Haw-Haw), broadcaster of Nazi propaganda, hanged.

•

1980 Joy Adamson, wildlife conservationist and author of *Born Free*, was murdered.

•

1981 Princess Alice, Countess of Athlone, the last survivor of Queen Victoria's 37 grandchildren, died aged 97.

•

1990 Panama's leader Manuel Noriega surrendered to US forces after ten days under siege in the Vatican Embassy.

4 JANUARY

1642 King Charles I entered Parliament with soldiers in a bid to arrest five MPs, sparking the English Civil War.

•

1643 Sir Isaac Newton, physicist and mathematician, was born.

•

1877 Cornelius Vanderbilt, financier and transport magnate whose steamship service flourished with the 1849 Gold Rush, died.

•

1948 after more than 100 years of British rule, Burma became an independent republic.

•

1951 Chinese Communist and North Korean troops captured Seoul during the Korean War.

•

1967 world speed record breaker Donald Campbell was killed in Bluebird on Coniston Water, Cumbria, during a record attempt.

5 JANUARY

1066 Edward the Confessor, King of England
since 1042, died.

•

1592 Shah Jahan, Mogul emperor of India, who ordered
the building of the Taj Mahal as a mausoleum for his wife,
was born.

•

1855 King Camp Gillette, inventor of his eponymous
safety razor, was born in Wisconsin.

•

1941 Amy Johnson, record-breaking aviator, died after
her aircraft crashed in the Thames estuary.

•

1968 Alexander Dubcek became First Secretary of
Czechoslovakia's Communist Party, ushering in the
Prague Spring.

•

1971 international one-day cricket was born when England
played Australia in Melbourne, the Test match having been
abandoned due to rain.

6 JANUARY

1066 Harold Godwinson was crowned King of England in succession to Edward the Confessor, prompting the Normans to invade.

1412 St Joan of Arc, French heroine, was born into a peasant family at Domrémy, (later called Domrémy-la-Pucelle) in the Vosges.

1681 the first recorded boxing match in the UK was arranged by the Duke of Albemarle between his butler and his butcher.

1838 in New Jersey, Samuel Morse gave the first public demonstration of his electric telegraph system.

1852 Louis Braille, who invented a reading and writing system for blind people, died in Paris.

7 JANUARY

1714 a patent was granted to the English engineer
Henry Mill for his typewriter design.

•

1785 Blanchard and Jeffries made the first hot-air balloon
crossing of the Channel.

•

1789 the first nationwide election was held in America,
with George Washington elected as president.

•

1827 Sandford Fleming, Scottish engineer who divided
the world into time zones, was born.

•

1955 Marian Anderson was placed under contract
by the Metropolitan Opera in New York, the first
African-American to be so engaged.

•

1999 the impeachment trial of President Clinton began
in Washington.

8 JANUARY

1337 Giotto, painter and architect, died in Florence.

1642 Galileo Galilei, mathematician and astronomer, died in Arcetri, Tuscany.

1742 Philip Astley, founder of Astley's Royal Amphitheatre, a forerunner of the modern circus, was born in Newcastle-under-Lyme.

1824 Wilkie Collins, author of *The Woman in White*, was born.

1897 Dennis Wheatley, historical novelist and thriller writer (*The Devil Rides Out*), was born.

1935 Elvis Presley, singer, was born in Tupelo, Mississippi.

1940 wartime rationing of butter, bacon and sugar began in the UK.

1959 Charles de Gaulle was proclaimed president of the French Republic.

1799 income tax was introduced by prime minister William Pitt the Younger to raise funds for the Napoleonic Wars.

•

1806 Horatio Nelson was buried in St Paul's Cathedral.

•

1816 Sir Humphry Davy's safety lamp was first used in a mine.

•

1873 Napoleon III, French Emperor, died in exile in England.

•

1913 Richard Nixon, president of the United States 1969–74, was born in Yorba Linda, California.

•

1960 work began on the Aswan High Dam in Egypt and would take ten years to complete.

•

1972 the liner *Queen Elizabeth* was destroyed by fire in Hong Kong harbour.

1840 the Penny Post was introduced.

•

1862 Samuel Colt, firearms manufacturer, died as one of America's wealthiest men.

•

1863 the Metropolitan Railway — ancestor of the London Underground — opened between Paddington and Farringdon Street.

•

1870 the Standard Oil Company, which was to be vastly enriched by the advent of the motor car, founded by William and John D Rockefeller.

•

1917 William Cody (Buffalo Bill), US army scout, and later showman who killed 4,280 buffalo in eight months to feed railroad workers, died.

•

1946 the inaugural session of the UN general assembly opened in London.

•

1985 Clive Sinclair launched the C5 electric car at £399.

11 JANUARY

1753 Sir Hans Sloane, whose collection was the foundation of the British Museum, died at Chelsea.

•

1891 Georges Haussmann, architect who planned much of modern Paris, died.

•

1922 insulin first used successfully in the treatment of diabetes.

•

1928 Thomas Hardy, author of *Tess of the d'Urbervilles*, died at Dorchester, Dorset.

•

1946 King Zog of Albania was dethroned.

•

1969 Richmal Crompton, author of *Just William*, died.

•

1973 the Open University awarded its first degrees.

•

1981 a three-man British team, led by Sir Ranulph Fiennes, completed the longest and fastest crossing of Antarctica after 75 days and 2,500 miles.

12 JANUARY

1628 Charles Perrault, author of fairytales (*Cinderella*, *The Sleeping Beauty*), was born in Paris.

•

1856 John Singer Sargent, portrait painter, was born in Florence.

•

1879 the British declared war on the Zulu leader Cetewayo.

•

1948 the London Co-op opened the first supermarket in the capital at Manor Park.

•

1950 64 submariners and dockyard workers were killed when the tanker *Divina* struck *Truculent* on the Thames.

•

1970 a Boeing 747 landed at Heathrow after its first flight from New York.

•

1976 Agatha Christie, crime novelist, died aged 85.

•

2010 316,000 people died in an earthquake in Haiti.

13 JANUARY

1893 the Independent Labour Party formed by Keir Hardie to promote working-class representation.

•

1906 Aleksandr Popov, who used radio waves to transmit a message in 1896, independently of Guglielmo Marconi, died in St Petersburg.

•

1929 Wyatt Earp, gambler and law officer involved in the gunfight at the OK Corral in 1881, died.

•

1941 James Joyce, novelist, died in Zurich aged 58.

1978 Nasa selected its first women astronauts.

•

1989 the Friday the 13th virus struck at IBM-compatible computers.

•

2004 Harold Shipman, who killed more than 250 people, hanged himself in prison.

14 JANUARY

1874 Johann Philipp Reis, whose telephone was not a commercial success, died.

•

1878 the first demonstration of Alexander Graham Bell's newly invented telephone given to Queen Victoria on the Isle of Wight.

•

1898 Rev Charles Dodgson (Lewis Carroll), author of *Alice's Adventures in Wonderland*, died.

•

1957 Humphrey Bogart, actor (*Casablanca*), died of cancer aged 57.

•

1977 Anthony Eden, prime minister 1955–57, died.

•

1983 Metropolitan Police officers shot and gravely injured film editor Stephen Waldorf, mistakenly believing him to be an escaped convict.

•

1989 Muslims in Bradford ritually burnt a copy of Salman Rushdie's *The Satanic Verses*.

15 JANUARY

1559 Elizabeth I crowned Queen of England.

•

1759 the British Museum opened at Montague House, London.

1815 Emma, Lady Hamilton, mistress of Lord Nelson, died in poverty at Calais.

•

1867 40 skaters drowned when the ice broke on Regent's Park lake, London.

•

1970 the Nigeria-Biafra war concluded with Biafra's surrender after the deaths of more than one million people.

1973 President Nixon halted US bombing in North Vietnam after peace talks in Paris.

•

2001 the Wikipedia website went online.

•

2009 US Airways Flight 1549 safely crash-landed in the Hudson River between New York and New Jersey.

16 JANUARY

1604 the Hampton Court Conference ended, in which King James I authorised a new translation of the Bible.

•

1920 prohibition of the sale of alcohol began in America.

•

1944 General Dwight D Eisenhower arrived in England as supreme commander of Allied forces in Europe.

•

1969 21-year-old student Jan Palach set fire to himself in Prague in protest at the Russian invasion of Czechoslovakia.

•

1970 Colonel Muammar Gaddafi became the leader of Libya, following a coup against King Idris.

•

1979 the Shah of Iran was forced into exile in Egypt.

17 JANUARY

1773 Captain Cook's Resolution crossed the Antarctic Circle, the first ship to do so.

•

1874 conjoined Thai-American brothers Chang and Eng Bunker, regarded as the original Siamese twins, died within two hours of one another, aged 62, in North Carolina.

•

1912 Captain Robert Scott reached the South Pole, to discover his rival Roald Amundsen had reached it first.

•

1983 the BBC introduced breakfast television.

•

1991 allied forces launched Operation Desert Storm against Iraqi positions following Saddam Hussein's invasion of Kuwait.

•

1995 more than 6,400 people were killed when an earthquake struck Kobe, Japan.

18 JANUARY

1778 Captain Cook sighted the Sandwich Islands (Hawaii).

1813 Joseph Farwell Glidden, farmer who patented the first commercially viable barbed wire, born in New Hampshire.

1871 William of Prussia was proclaimed the first German Emperor.

1882 AA Milne, children's writer, was born.

1884 Arthur Ransome, children's writer, was born.

1911 piloted by Lt Eugene B Ely, the first aircraft to land on a ship touched down on the cruiser USS *Pennsylvania* in San Francisco harbour.

1919 the Versailles Peace Conference opened.

1989 Bruce Chatwin, travel writer (*In Patagonia*) and novelist, died in Nice aged 48.

19 JANUARY

1736 James Watt, designer of the steam engine that largely powered the Industrial Revolution, was born in Greenock, Renfrewshire.

•

1813 Sir Henry Bessemer, inventor of a steel production process that reduced the alloy's price to a fifth of its former cost, was born in Charlton, Hertfordshire.

•

1915 in the first air raid on Britain, a German zeppelin crossed the Norfolk coast and bombed Great Yarmouth and King's Lynn.

•

1937 aviator Howard Hughes set a new record by flying from Los Angeles to New York in 7 hours and 28 minutes.

•

1966 Indira Gandhi became India's first woman prime minister.

1841 Britain and China signed the Convention of Chuanbi, which ceded Hong Kong to the British.

•

1900 RD Blackmore, novelist (*Lorna Doone*), died.

•

1900 John Ruskin, art critic, died.

•

1942 Reinhard Heydrich chaired the Wannsee Conference in Berlin, which established the framework for the final solution to the Jewish question.

•

1972 unemployment in the UK rose above one million for the first time since the 1930s.

•

1987 Terry Waite, the Archbishop of Canterbury's special envoy in Lebanon, was kidnapped in Beirut.

•

1993 Audrey Hepburn, actress (*Roman Holiday, My Fair Lady*), died aged 63.

1790 Dr Joseph-Ignace Guillotin proposed the guillotine to the newly formed National Assembly of Paris as a humane method of execution.

·

1793 King Louis XVI of France was executed (by guillotine).

·

1907 taxi cabs were officially recognised in Britain.

·

1911 the first Monte Carlo car rally began.

·

1924 Lenin (Vladimir Ilyich Ulyanov), Russian revolutionary, died at Gorki, Moscow, aged 53.

·

1950 George Orwell (Eric Blair), essayist and novelist, died aged 46.

·

1954 the first nuclear-powered submarine, the USS *Nautilus*, was launched.

·

1976 Concorde made its inaugural commercial flight, from London to Bahrain in 3hr 37min.

22 JANUARY

1440 Ivan III, the Great, whose conquests created a consolidated Russian state, was born.

•

1666 Shah Jahan, Mughal emperor of India, died.

•

1788 George Gordon Byron (6th Baron Byron), poet, was born.

•

1901 Queen Victoria, Britain's monarch since 1837, died.

•

1905 Russian troops fired on marching workers in St Petersburg, killing more than 500 in the first Bloody Sunday.

•

1924 Ramsay MacDonald became Britain's first Labour prime minister.

•

1944 the Allied landings began in Anzio, Italy.

•

1946 President Truman established the Central Intelligence Group, from which, two years later, the CIA was created.

23 JANUARY

1790 Fletcher Christian and the *Bounty*'s other mutineers landed on Pitcairn Island.

•

1806 William Pitt the Younger, prime minister 1783–1801 and 1804–06, died aged 46.

•

1837 John Field, Irish composer who created the piano nocturne, died in Moscow.

•

1883 Gustave Doré, graphic artist who illustrated such works as Dante's *Divine Comedy*, died.

•

1943 Tripoli was captured by British forces under Field Marshal Montgomery.

•

1985 the proceedings of the House of Lords were televised for the first time.

•

1989 surrealist painter Salvador Dalí died in Figueres, Spain, aged 84.

24 JANUARY

41 Gaius Caesar (Caligula), Roman Emperor from 37, was murdered.

1664 Sir John Vanbrugh, soldier, playwright and architect of Blenheim Palace, died.

1712 Frederick the Great, King of Prussia 1740–86 , born in Berlin.

1895 Lord Randolph Churchill, statesman and father of Sir Winston, died aged 45.

1965 Sir Winston Churchill, prime minister 1940–45 and 1951–55, died aged 90.

1972 a Japanese soldier, Shoichi Yokoi, was discovered on Guam, 28 years after the Japanese surrender, believing that the Second World War was still in progress.

1984 the Apple Macintosh personal computer went on sale.

25 JANUARY

1533 King Henry VIII married Anne Boleyn in secret.

•

1640 Robert Burton, author of *The Anatomy of Melancholy*, died.

•

1759 Robert Burns, Scottish poet whose popularity is reaffirmed in the Burns Night celebrations, was born in Alloway, Ayr.

•

1919 the League of Nations was founded to resolve international disputes.

•

1924 the first Winter Olympics began in Chamonix, France.

•

1947 gangster Al Capone died at home of a heart attack.

•

1971 Idi Amin deposed the Ugandan president Milton Obote.

•

1990 Benazir Bhutto, the prime minister of Pakistan, became the first head of government to give birth.

1790 *Così fan tutte* by Wolfgang Amadeus Mozart was first performed in Vienna.

•

1824 Théodore Géricault, painter who used corpses in the morgue as models for *The Raft of the Medusa*, died.

•

1855 Gérard de Nerval, French Romantic poet who kept a lobster as a pet, died.

•

1885 General Charles Gordon was killed at Khartoum during the rising led by the Mahdi.

•

1905 the largest diamond in the world, the Cullinan, was mined at Pretoria, South Africa.

•

1950 India became a republic within the Commonwealth.

•

1998 President Bill Clinton denied having had sexual relations with intern Monica Lewinsky.

27 JANUARY

1302 Dante Alighieri was expelled from Florence for his political activities, and while in exile wrote his masterpiece, *The Divine Comedy*.

•

1880 the American inventor Thomas Alva Edison was granted a patent for his electric incandescent lamp.

•

1944 Leningrad (now St Petersburg) was relieved after a 28-month siege.

•

1945 the Soviet army liberated 5,000 inmates of Auschwitz concentration camp in Poland.

•

1967 Virgil Grissom, Ed White and Roger Chafee, astronauts, died after an electrical fault ignited pure oxygen in their *Apollo 1* spacecraft.

•

1972 Mahalia Jackson, the "Queen of Gospel", died.

28 JANUARY

814 Charlemagne, Holy Roman Emperor since 800, died aged 71.

•

1547 King Henry VIII, who had reigned since 1509, died aged 55.

•

1596 Sir Francis Drake, English admiral and circumnavigator of the globe, died aged 55 at Portobelo, Panama.

•

1807 London's Pall Mall became the first street in the world illuminated by gaslight.

•

1896 the first speeding fine was imposed on a British motorist for exceeding 2mph in a built-up area.

•

1986 the space shuttle *Challenger* exploded shortly after lift-off and its crew of five men and two women were killed.

29 JANUARY

1819 Sir Thomas Stamford Raffles landed in Singapore, with it becoming a British colony five years later.

•

1820 King George III, who had reigned since 1760, died aged 81.

•

1856 the Victoria Cross was established by royal warrant to honour acts of valour during the Crimean War.

•

1860 Anton Chekhov, playwright, was born in Taganrog, Russia.

•

1886 Karl Benz patented the first automobile.

•

1942 *Desert Island Discs* was first broadcast by the BBC.

•

1996 Venice's opera house, fatefully named La Fenice (The Phoenix), was completely destroyed by fire, suspected to be arson.

1649 King Charles I, who had reigned since 1625, was executed in Whitehall.

•

1661 Oliver Cromwell was ritually executed, more than two years after his death.

•

1790 the first lifeboat was tested by Henry Greathead of South Shields.

•

1933 Hitler was sworn in as German chancellor.

•

1948 Mahatma Gandhi, Indian leader, was assassinated in Delhi.

•

1965 Sir Winston Churchill's state funeral took place in London.

•

1968 the Vietcong launched the Tet Offensive against South Vietnam.

•

1972 British troops killed 13 people during a civil rights march in Londonderry on what is now known as Bloody Sunday.

1606 Guy Fawkes and his fellow Gunpowder Plot conspirators were executed.

•

1788 Charles Edward Stuart (Bonnie Prince Charlie), leader of the Jacobite rebellion, died in Rome aged 68.

•

1858 the *Great Eastern* steamship, the largest vessel in the world, built by Isambard Kingdom Brunel, was launched.

•

1929 Leon Trotsky was expelled from the Soviet Union.

•

1983 the wearing of front seatbelts in cars was made compulsory in Britain.

•

1990 the first McDonald's restaurant in Russia opened in Pushkin Square, Moscow.

•

2010 *Avatar* became the first film to gross more than $2 billion worldwide.

1 FEBRUARY

1851 Mary Shelley, who at 21 wrote *Frankenstein,* died aged 54.

•

1874 Hugo von Hofmannsthal, poet, dramatist and librettist (*Der Rosenkavalier*), was born in Vienna.

1884 publication of the first fascicle of the *Oxford English Dictionary*.

•

1896 the world premiere of Puccini's opera *La Bohème* took place in Turin, with Arturo Toscanini conducting.

1910 the first British labour exchange opened.

•

1915 Stanley Matthews, footballer, was born in Stoke-on-Trent.

•

1924 Britain formally recognised the Soviet Union.

•

1974 Ronald Biggs, one of the Great Train Robbers, was arrested by Brazilian police in Rio de Janeiro.

2 FEBRUARY

1650 Nell Gwyn, comic actress and mistress of
King Charles II, was born.

•

1709 Scottish sailor Alexander Selkirk, inspiration
for Robinson Crusoe, was rescued after being marooned
for four years on an island off Chile.

1901 the state funeral of Queen Victoria took place
at Windsor.

•

1972 the British embassy in Dublin was burnt down by
demonstrators protesting the killings on Bloody Sunday
two days previously in Londonderry.

•

1977 the Pompidou Centre opened in Paris.

•

1979 Sid Vicious (Simon John Ritchie), bass guitarist
of the Sex Pistols, died in New York aged 21.

3 FEBRUARY

1761 Richard (Beau) Nash, dandy who developed Bath into the most fashionable spa town in England, died.

•

1877 *The Celebrated Chop Waltz*, better known as *Chopsticks*, music for the piano by 16-year-old Euphemia Allen, was registered at the British Museum.

•

1919 President Woodrow Wilson attended the first meeting of the League of Nations in Paris.

•

1924 Woodrow Wilson, 28th American president 1913–21, died aged 67.

•

1960 Harold Macmillan made his Wind of Change speech to the South African parliament.

•

1969 Yassir Arafat was appointed chairman of the Palestine Liberation Organisation.

1911 Rolls-Royce commissioned its famous figurehead, *The Spirit of Ecstasy*, from the sculptor Charles Sykes.

•

1927 Malcolm Campbell set the land-speed record at 174.88mph in his 12-cylinder Napier-Campbell Blue Bird on Pendine Sands, Carmarthen Bay.

•

1945 the Yalta conference opened, at which Churchill, Roosevelt and Stalin discussed strategy for the final months of the war.

•

1962 *The Sunday Times* issued the first colour supplement in Britain.

•

1968 the world's largest hovercraft (165 tons and costing £1.75 million) was launched at Cowes, Isle of Wight.

•

1971 the British carmaker Rolls-Royce declared itself bankrupt.

1811 the Prince of Wales, later King George IV, was declared Prince Regent.

•

1887 Verdi's *Otello* received its world premiere at the Teatro alla Scala, Milan.

•

1920 the RAF College at Cranwell, Lincolnshire, opened.

•

1982 Laker Airways collapsed with debts of £270 million.

•

1983 the Nazi war criminal Klaus Barbie was imprisoned in France.

•

1987 Liberace, pianist known for his flamboyant costumes, died.

•

1999 South African president Nelson Mandela made his last State of the Nation speech to parliament before retiring.

•

2008 tornados killed 57 people in the southern United States.

6 FEBRUARY

1685 King James II acceded to the throne.

•

1919 William Rossetti, writer and brother to Christina and Dante Gabriel, died.

•

1945 Bob Marley, singer-songwriter, was born in Nine Mile, Jamaica.

•

1952 Queen Elizabeth II acceded to the throne while visiting Kenya.

•

1958 seven members of the Manchester United football team were among those killed in an air crash in Munich.

•

1964 France and Britain agreed to build a Channel tunnel.

•

1971 astronaut Alan Shepard became the first person to hit a golf ball on the moon.

7 FEBRUARY

1812 Charles Dickens, novelist and social critic, was born in Portsmouth.

•

1863 HMS *Orpheus* was wrecked off New Zealand, killing 185 sailors.

•

1940 Disney's film *Pinocchio* was given a gala premiere in New York.

•

1971 Swiss men voted to allow women to vote in federal elections and to stand for parliament.

•

1974 prime minister Edward Heath called a snap election.

•

1992 ministers from the 12 European Community countries signed the Maastricht treaty.

•

2005 Ellen MacArthur completed her single-handed round-the-world voyage in the record-breaking time of 71 days 14 hours and 18 minutes.

8 FEBRUARY

1587 Mary Queen of Scots was executed at Fotheringhay Castle, Northamptonshire, aged 44.

•

1725 Peter the Great, tsar of Russia since 1682, died aged 52.

•

1872 Robert Southwell Bourke (6th Earl of Mayo), Viceroy of India, was assassinated in the Andaman Islands.

•

1924 the gas chamber was first used as a form of execution when Gee Jon was put to death in Nevada for murder.

•

1965 a ban was announced on cigarette advertising on British television.

•

1983 Shergar, the Aga Khan's Derby winner, was kidnapped from stables in Co Kildare and, despite a ransom demand, was never seen again.

1540 the first recorded race meeting in England was held at Roodee Fields, Chester.

•

1567 Lord Darnley, consort of Mary Queen of Scots, was murdered in Edinburgh.

•

1933 ten days after Hitler had become German chancellor, members of the Oxford Union voted against fighting for "King and Country".

•

1972 the British government declared a state of emergency after a month-long miners' strike.

•

1979 Trevor Francis became the first British footballer to break the £1m transfer fee when he signed for Nottingham Forest.

•

1996 an IRA bomb exploded in London's Docklands, killing two and injuring 100.

1355 the St Scholastica's Day riot began in Oxford,
with opposing forces of town and gown on the rampage
for three days.

•

1837 Alexander Pushkin, Russian writer, died following
a duel with his wife's admirer.

•

1931 ceremonies began to inaugurate New Delhi as the
capital of India (in place of Delhi).

•

1962 Gary Powers, the US pilot of a U2 spy plane shot down
over the Soviet Union in 1960, was exchanged in Berlin for
a KGB agent.

•

1964 the Great St Bernard Tunnel under the Alps between
Switzerland and Italy was opened to traffic.

1852 the first flushing public lavatory for women opened in Bedford Street, London.

•

1858 a 14-year-old French girl, Bernadette Soubirous, claimed that a beautiful lady, later identified as the Virgin Mary, appeared to her near Lourdes.

•

1878 the first weekly weather report was issued by the Meteorological Office.

•

1975 Margaret Thatcher became the first woman leader of a British political party.

•

1977 the heaviest recorded crustacean, a lobster weighing 44lb 6oz, was caught off Nova Scotia in Canada.

•

1990 Nelson Mandela was released from prison in South Africa after 27 years in captivity.

12 FEBRUARY

1554 Lady Jane Grey, Queen of England for nine days, was executed aged 16.

•

1809 Charles Darwin, naturalist, was born in Shrewsbury.

•

1809 Abraham Lincoln, 16th president of the US, was born in Hodgenville, Kentucky.

•

1818 Chile proclaimed its independence from Spain.

•

1912 Hsuan-t'ung (Pu-Yi), the last emperor of China, was forced to abdicate.

•

1924 Calvin Coolidge became the first US president to deliver a political speech on radio.

•

1986 the Channel Tunnel treaty was signed between United Kingdom and France.

•

2001 *NEAR Shoemaker* touched down on 433 Eros, becoming the first spacecraft to land on an asteroid.

13 FEBRUARY

1542 Catherine Howard, the fifth wife of Henry VIII, was executed for adultery.

•

1601 John Lancaster led the first East India Company voyage from London.

•

1689 William III and Mary II acceded to the throne of England.

•

1692 the MacDonalds were massacred by the Campbells at Glencoe.

•

1917 the spy Mata Hari was arrested by the French.

•

1945 Dresden was devastated when RAF bombers attacked the city.

•

1959 the Barbie doll went on sale.

•

1960 France exploded its first atomic bomb.

14 FEBRUARY

1477 John Paston received the first recorded valentine letter in English, from Margery Brews.

·

1838 Margaret Knight, inventor of the square-bottom paper bag, was born in York, Maine.

·

1852 the Great Ormond Street Hospital for Children, fitted with ten beds, admitted its first patient, George Parr, who was suffering from catarrh and diarrhoea.

·

1895 Oscar Wilde's final play, *The Importance of Being Earnest*, opened in London.

·

1922 Marconi began regular broadcasting transmissions from Writtle in Essex.

·

1939 the German battleship *Bismarck* was launched at Hamburg.

·

2005 three PayPal workers started a video-sharing website, calling it YouTube.

1882 the first cargo of frozen meat left New Zealand for Britain on the SS *Dunedin*.

•

1942 Singapore surrendered to Japanese forces.

•

1944 the Allies bombed Monte Cassino monastery in Italy to prevent the Germans fortifying it.

•

1965 Canada flew its newly adopted red maple leaf flag for the first time.

•

1965 Nat King Cole, singer and jazz pianist who sold more than 50 million records, died of cancer aged 45.

•

1971 Britain adopted decimal currency.

16 FEBRUARY

1659 the first known British cheque (for £400) was written by Nicholas Vanacker.

•

1824 the first meeting of the Athenaeum Club — for "Literary and Scientific men and followers of the Fine Arts" — took place in London.

•

1923 the archaeologist Howard Carter entered the sealed burial chamber of Tutankhamun in Thebes, Egypt. (The ruins of Thebes are found within the modern city of Luxor.)

•

1959 Fidel Castro became prime minister of Cuba, and would govern until 2008.

•

1960 the US nuclear submarine *Triton* set off on the first underwater round-the-world voyage.

•

1998 the *Angel of the North,* a sculpture by Antony Gormley, was unveiled in Gateshead.

17 FEBRUARY

1600 the philosopher Giordano Bruno was burnt at the stake in Rome for heresies including maintaining that Earth was not the only inhabited planet.

•

1818 German inventor Baron Karl von Drais de Sauerbrun patented the draisine, forerunner of the bicycle.

•

1864 AB (Banjo) Paterson, poet (*Waltzing Matilda*), was born in Orange, New South Wales.

1880 Tsar Alexander II of Russia survived an assassination attempt when a bomb exploded at the Winter Palace, St Petersburg.

•

1909 Geronimo, Apache leader, died in captivity aged 79.

•

1972 the House of Commons voted to join the European Common Market.

18 FEBRUARY

1478 George, Duke of Clarence, brother of Edward IV and Richard III, was said to have been drowned in a butt of malmsey at the Tower of London.

•

1678 John Bunyan's *The Pilgrim's Progress* was published, much of it having been composed while he was in prison for illegal preaching.

•

1929 the winners of the first Academy Awards (known as Oscars from 1931) were announced, with the presentation being held later that year. (See 16 May.)

•

1930 Pluto was discovered by the American astronomer Clyde W Tombaugh.

•

1979 snow fell in the Sahara Desert.

•

2005 a law banning hunting with dogs came into force in England and Wales.

1473 Nicolaus Copernicus, astronomer who proposed
that the sun not the Earth was the centre of the Universe,
was born in Poland.

•

1861 Tsar Alexander II abolished serfdom in Russia.

•

1878 the patent for Thomas Edison's phonograph
(the original gramophone) was issued.

•

1897 the Women's Institute was founded by Adelaide
Hoodless in Ontario, Canada, and came to Britain during
the First World War.

•

1945 US marines landed on the island of Iwo Jima, whose
capture created a forward air base in the war against Japan.

•

1985 the BBC televised the first episode of *EastEnders*.

1632 Thomas Osborne (1st Duke of Leeds), statesman and leader of the Tories who was imprisoned twice on charges of bribery, was born.

•

1811 Austria declared itself bankrupt because of the cost of fighting Napoleon.

•

1816 the opening night of Rossini's opera *The Barber of Seville* was a fiasco, with one performer singing an aria with a bleeding nose after tripping on a trapdoor, and a cat attacking another during the finale to the first act.

•

1947 Viscount Mountbatten of Burma was appointed last viceroy of India.

•

1962 John Glenn became the first American to orbit the Earth.

1741 Jethro Tull, inventor of the more efficient
horse-drawn seed-drill, died at Hungerford, Berks.

•

1862 Nathaniel Gordon became the only American
to be executed for slave trading, their shipping being
illegal under the 1820 Piracy Act.

•

1916 the ten-month-long Battle of Verdun began
with nine hours of the heaviest artillery bombardment
ever witnessed.

•

1964 24,000 rolls of Beatles wallpaper were flown
to America.

•

1965 Malcolm X was assassinated in New York aged 39
by three members of the Nation of Islam.

•

1972 President Nixon began his historic visit
of rapprochement to China.

22 FEBRUARY

1878 Frank Woolworth opened his first store in Utica, New York.

•

1897 Blondin (Jean-François Gravelet), acrobat and tightrope walker known for his crossing of Niagara Falls, died at Ealing, London, aged 72.

•

1907 taxi cabs with meters were introduced in London.

•

1928 Bert Hinkler completed the first solo flight from England to Australia, landing in Darwin having taken off from Croydon 15 days earlier.

•

1946 Dr Selman Abraham Waksman announced his discovery of the antibiotic streptomycin.

•

2006 £53 million was discovered to have been stolen from a Securitas depot in Kent, in Britain's biggest robbery.

1633 Samuel Pepys, diarist, was born in London.

•

1820 the Cato Street Conspiracy, a plot to assassinate the entire British cabinet, was uncovered.

•

1821 John Keats, poet, died in Rome of tuberculosis aged 25.

•

1874 Major Walter Clopton Wingfield patented his new game of lawn tennis.

•

1889 Victor Fleming, director whose films included *Gone with the Wind* and *The Wizard of Oz* (both 1939), was born in California.

•

1905 the world's first Rotary Club was founded in Chicago.

•

1997 it was announced that Dolly, the world's first cloned sheep, had been born.

1582 Pope Gregory XIII published a papal bull that established a new-style (Gregorian) calendar, but it took England almost 200 years to follow suit.

•

1848 the last king of France, Louis-Philippe, who had reigned since 1830, was forced to abdicate by revolutionaries who then proclaimed the Second Republic.

•

1920 US-born MP Nancy Astor became the first woman to speak in the House of Commons.

•

1923 the *Flying Scotsman* entered service with the London and North Eastern Railway.

•

2001 Claude Shannon, mathematician whose work on modern information theory laid the basis for the information age, died.

1570 Pope Pius V excommunicated the Protestant Queen Elizabeth I.

•

1836 Samuel Colt was granted a patent for his revolver.

•

1862 a paper currency known as Greenbacks was introduced in the US by order of President Abraham Lincoln.

•

1868 Andrew Johnson, 17th American president, was impeached, to be acquitted the following May by a single vote.

•

1952 the Windscale plutonium plant at Sellafield began operation.

•

1964 floating like a butterfly, stinging like a bee, Cassius Clay (later Muhammad Ali) won the world heavyweight boxing championship when Sonny Liston failed to come out for the seventh round.

1797 the Bank of England issued £1 banknotes for the first time.

•

1815 Napoleon escaped from exile in Elba.

•

1848 *The Communist Manifesto* was published, having been printed in London.

•

1924 Adolf Hitler appeared in court, charged with treason for leading the failed coup d'état known as the beer-hall putsch.

•

1935 a Heyford bomber flying in the main beam of a BBC short-wave transmitter gave back reflected signals to the ground, winning Robert Watson-Watt government approval to develop radar technology.

•

1936 Hitler opened the first factory to manufacture the Volkswagen, the people's car.

27 FEBRUARY

c. 272 Constantine the Great, Roman emperor 306–337, was born in modern Nis, Serbia.

•

1814 Beethoven's 8th Symphony received its premiere in Vienna.

•

1879 at Johns Hopkins University, Baltimore, Maryland, Constantin Fahlberg and Ira Remsen accidentally discovered saccharin.

•

1900 a meeting of trade unionists, Marxists and Fabians resulted in the foundation of the Labour Representation Committee, or British Labour Party.

•

1902 John Steinbeck, novelist, was born in Salinas, California.

•

1933 arson destroyed part of Germany's Reichstag building, leading to the suspension of civil liberties.

•

1939 General Franco's rebel Nationalist Government was recognised by Britain and France.

28 FEBRUARY

1533 Michel de Montaigne, philosopher who popularised the essay form, was born.

•

1900 after a four-month siege during the Boer War, the 20,000-strong British garrison in Ladysmith was relieved.

•

1922 Lord Allenby, high commissioner in Egypt, announced the termination of the British protectorate and the inception of Egyptian independence.

•

1956 Jay Forrester patented random-access coincident-current magnetic storage, which would become the standard memory device for computers.

•

1975 a London Underground train crashed at Moorgate station, killing 35 people.

•

1986 the Swedish prime minister Olof Palme was assassinated while walking home in Stockholm, a crime that remains unsolved.

29 FEBRUARY

1868 Conservative Party leader Benjamin Disraeli formed his first government.

•

1880 the 9.3-mile St Gotthard railway tunnel, then the longest in the world, was completed, linking Switzerland and Italy.

•

1940 Hattie McDaniel became the first African-American actress to win an Oscar, for *Gone With the Wind.*

•

1956 Pakistan became an Islamic republic.

•

1960 thousands of people were killed in an earthquake in Agadir, Morocco.

•

1960 Hugh Hefner opened the first Playboy Club in Chicago.

•

1984 Pierre Trudeau resigned after 15 years as premier of Canada.

•

1996 the siege of Sarajevo ended after almost seven years.

1360 during the siege of Rheims, King Edward III contributed £16 towards the ransom of Geoffrey Chaucer, then serving as a soldier.

•

1872 US president Ulysses S Grant established America's first national park, Yellowstone.

•

1912 George Grossmith, co-author of *The Diary of a Nobody* and the comic lead in Gilbert and Sullivan's early productions, died.

•

1932 Charles Augustus, the 20-month-old son of the American aviator Charles Lindbergh, was abducted from his nursery and later found dead.

•

1966 the unmanned Soviet probe *Venera 3* impacted on Venus, becoming the first spacecraft to land on another planet.

2 MARCH

1882 Queen Victoria narrowly escaped assassination by
Roderick Maclean as she sat in her railway carriage at
Windsor station, this being the eighth attempt made
on her life since the start of her reign.

•

1949 Captain James Gallagher and his US air force crew
completed the first round-the-world non-stop flight
(23,452 miles in 94 hours and 1 minute).

•

1956 Morocco declared its political independence
from France.

•

1958 the British Trans-Antarctic Expedition, led by
Dr Vivian Fuchs, completed the first surface crossing
of Antarctica.

•

1970 Ian Smith, the Rhodesian prime minister, declared
his country an independent republic.

3 MARCH

1875 the first performance of *Carmen* at Paris's Opéra-Comique was so poorly received that it was thought to have hastened the death of its composer, Georges Bizet.

•

1894 six months after his second Home Rule Bill had been defeated by the House of Lords, William Gladstone resigned as prime minister.

•

1924 Turkish president Mustafa Kemal Atatürk abolished the caliphate (the Islamic leadership of the Ottoman sultans).

•

1931 the US Congress adopted *The Star-Spangled Banner* as the American national anthem.

•

1991 Rodney King was filmed being beaten by Los Angeles police officers, leading to widespread riots.

4 MARCH

1461 King Henry VI was deposed by his cousin Edward, Duke of York (who became King Edward IV).

•

1789 the Congress of the United States held its first meeting in New York.

•

1824 the National Institution for the Preservation of Life from Shipwreck was founded (from 1854, the Royal National Lifeboat Institution).

•

1890 the last of eight million rivets holding together 55,000 tons of steel was driven home at the opening ceremony of the Forth Bridge.

•

1966 the *London Evening Standard* published an interview with John Lennon in which he claimed the Beatles were more popular than Jesus.

5 MARCH

1933 in the last elections in a unified Germany until 1990, Adolf Hitler's National Socialist Party won 44 per cent of the seats.

•

1936 for eight minutes, the Spitfire made its maiden flight from Eastleigh aerodrome.

•

1946 at a speech in Missouri, Winston Churchill declared: "From Stettin in the Baltic to Trieste in the Adriatic, an iron curtain has descended across the Continent."

•

1956 the US Supreme Court upheld a ban on racial segregation in schools and universities.

•

1973 68 people were killed when two Spanish aircraft collided over France, where air traffic controllers were on strike.

6 MARCH

1831 Edgar Allan Poe was expelled from West Point Military Academy for non-attendance at chapel.

•

1836 after a 13-day siege, a garrison of 187 Texans was wiped out by 3,000 Mexicans at the Battle of the Alamo.

•

1899 aspirin was patented by Felix Hoffmann.

•

1930 the first collection of frozen vegetables, fruit, fish and meat was released for sale by Clarence Birdseye.

•

1974 the miners' strike ended after the Labour government offered a pay rise of 35 per cent.

•

1987 193 people died when the ferry *Herald of Free Enterprise* capsized outside Zeebrugge.

7 MARCH

1274 St Thomas Aquinas, theologian, died in the Cistercian monastery at Fossanova, Italy.

•

1804 the Royal Horticultural Society was founded at the bookshop of James Hatchard, Piccadilly.

•

1912 three months after becoming the first to reach the South Pole, Roald Amundsen arrived in Tasmania and was able to tell his brother the news.

•

1918 the Bolsheviks changed their name to the Russian Communist Party.

•

1965 state troopers in Alabama attacked a civil rights march from Selma to Montgomery, injuring 50 people.

•

1987 Sunil Gavaskar, of India, became the first batsman to score 10,000 runs in Test cricket.

8 MARCH

1702 upon the death of her brother-in-law King William III, Queen Anne acceded to the throne.

•

1782 after claiming to have found evidence of the murder of white settlers, Pennsylvania militiamen massacred 90 native American Christians in Gnadenhutten, Ohio.

•

1917 Count Ferdinand von Zeppelin, airship constructor, died in Berlin.

•

1917 the February Revolution (so called because of the old-style calendar used in Russia) began with rioting at Petrograd (now St Petersburg).

•

1957 the Suez Canal was reopened after the departure of Israeli troops.

•

1965 3,500 US marines, the first American combat troops to land in Vietnam, were met by sightseers and girls proffering garlands.

9 MARCH

1741 British Admiral Edward Vernon began his assault
on the Spanish town of Cartagena (in modern Colombia),
but was eventually defeated.

•

1796 Napoleon Bonaparte married Joséphine de Beauharnais.

•

1956 British police deported Archbishop Makarios from
Cyprus to the Seychelles on charges of fostering terrorism.

•

1959 a doll called Barbara Millicent Roberts — Barbie for
short — was exhibited for the first time at the American
International Toy Fair.

•

1967 Joseph Stalin's daughter defected to the West,
requesting asylum at the US embassy in India.

•

1973 the people of Northern Ireland voted to remain within
the UK in a referendum.

10 MARCH

1831 the French Foreign Legion was founded, with its headquarters in Algeria.

•

1863 with the four-year-old future Kaiser Wilhelm II as a noticeably undisciplined wedding guest, the Prince of Wales (later King Edward VII) married Princess Alexandra of Denmark at St George's Chapel, Windsor.

•

1914 the suffragette Mary Richardson wielded an axe to slash Velázquez's *The Rokeby Venus* in the National Gallery.

•

1926 the future novelist Graham Greene began work as a home sub-editor on *The Times*.

•

1969 James Earl Ray was sentenced in Memphis, Tennessee, to 99 years in prison for the murder of Martin Luther King.

11 MARCH

1702 *The Daily Courant*, England's first daily national newspaper, was published near Fleet Street.

•

1749 Lorenzo Da Ponte, who wrote the libretti for three of Mozart's operas, was born in Ceneda (now Vittorio Veneto), Italy.

•

1811 the Luddite riots began as textile workers protested against newly developed labour-replacing machinery.

•

1941 the Lend-Lease Act gave the US president Franklin D Roosevelt the power to sell, transfer, exchange or lend equipment to any country to help it to defend itself against Axis powers.

•

1985 Mikhail Gorbachev became leader of the Soviet Union.

•

2004 193 people were killed in the Madrid train bombings.

12 MARCH

1894 Coca-Cola, originally invented as a cure for morphine addiction, was bottled and sold for the first time, by Joseph A Biedenharn.

1929 Asa Candler, who acquired the formula for Coca-Cola in 1888 and successfully marketed the drink, died in Atlanta, Georgia.

1930 Gandhi started his 300-mile march to the sea, in protest against British monopoly on the production of salt.

1938 Germany annexed Austria.

1984 Britain's miners went on strike over pit closures.

1993 257 people were killed in a series of 12 bombings in Mumbai.

1994 the Church of England ordained its first women priests.

1781 William Herschel discovered that Uranus was a planet, rather than the star that it was previously believed to be.

•

1855 Percival Lowell, who in 1915 postulated the existence of Planet X (Pluto), was born in Boston, Massachussetts.

•

1930 the Lowell Observatory in Arizona announced the astronomer Clyde Tombaugh's discovery of the planet Pluto.

•

1943 German forces under Amon Goeth liquidated the last 8,000 Jews from the ghetto in Krakow, Poland, its pre-war population having been 90,000.

•

1996 Thomas Hamilton shot dead 16 schoolchildren and their teacher, before turning the gun on himself in Dunblane, Scotland.

14 MARCH

1757 John Byng, British admiral, was executed in Portsmouth for failing to relieve Minorca.

•

1794 Eli Whitney was granted a patent for his cotton gin, which efficiently separated cotton fibres from their seeds, revolutionising life in the southern United States.

•

1883 Karl Marx, economic theorist who co-wrote *The Communist Manifesto*, died in London.

•

1885 *The Mikado*, by Gilbert and Sullivan, opened at the Savoy Theatre.

•

1915 the Royal Navy sank the German cruiser *Dresden* off Chile.

•

1942 Anne Miller became the first patient in the US successfully treated with penicillin.

•

2013 Xi Jinping appointed president of China.

15 MARCH

44 BC Julius Caesar, Roman general who assumed dictatorial power after his defeat of Pompey, was murdered in Rome.

•

1649 John Milton was appointed as Oliver Cromwell's secretary for foreign tongues, charged with composing the Commonwealth's correspondence (in Latin) to other powers.

•

1909 Harry Gordon Selfridge opened the first department store in London.

•

1917 Nicholas II, the last Russian tsar, abdicated.

•

1964 Elizabeth Taylor and Richard Burton married each other for the first time.

•

1991 the Birmingham Six were released after the Court of Appeal quashed their convictions for the murder of 21 people in two pub bombings.

16 MARCH

1872 at the Kennington Oval, the Wanderers beat
the Royal Engineers 1–0 in the first FA Cup final.

•

1940 James Isbister became the first Briton killed
in an air raid in the Second World War during an attack
on Scapa Flow, in the Orkney Islands.

•

1968 American forces massacred hundreds of Vietnamese
civilians at My Lai.

•

1978 the supertanker *Amoco Cadiz* split in two after running
aground in Brittany, causing what was then the largest
oil spill in history.

•

1988 thousands were killed in a poison gas attack
on Halabja, a Kurdish city in northern Iraq.

17 MARCH

180 Marcus Aurelius, Rome's emperor since 161, died.

•

1861 Victor Emmanuel II was proclaimed first king
of a united Italy.

•

1921 Dr Marie Stopes opened Britain's first birth control
clinic in North London.

•

1957 British European Airways withdrew its Viscount
aircraft from service after one of them crashed at
Manchester, killing 22 people.

•

1968 more than 300 people were arrested during an anti-
Vietnam War protest outside the US embassy in London.

•

1969 Golda Meir became the first woman prime minister
of Israel.

•

1978 thousands of Palestinians fled southern Lebanon
after a third day of Israeli attacks.

18 MARCH

1871 the Commune insurrection began in Paris.

•

1937 300 people, mostly children, were killed in an explosion at the New London school, Texas.

•

1965 Aleksei Leonov became the first person to walk in space.

•

1967 the oil tanker *Torrey Canyon* ran aground off Cornwall.

•

1990 thieves disguised as police officers stole paintings worth about £215 million from a gallery in Boston in the largest art heist in American history.

•

1992 white South Africans voted to end apartheid and create a multiracial government.

•

2015 gunmen attacked the Bardo Museum, Tunisia, killing 23 people, most of them tourists.

1834 six agricultural labourers from Tolpuddle, Dorchester, were sentenced to seven years' penal labour in Australia for what was in effect a new crime: forming a trade union.

•

1847 John Chapman, better known as Johnny Appleseed, wandering orchard-planter, died at Fort Wayne, Indiana.

•

1877 at Melbourne, Australia beat England by 45 runs in the first ever Test match.

•

1932 Sydney Harbour Bridge was officially opened.

•

1937 Pope Pius XI published the encyclical *On Atheistic Communism*, condemning bolshevistic and atheistic communism.

•

1982 the Argentine flag was raised at South Georgia in the Falkland Islands.

20 MARCH

1815 Napoleon Bonaparte returned to Paris at the start of his last Hundred Days as emperor.

•

1852 Harriet Beecher Stowe's novel *Uncle Tom's Cabin* was published.

•

1966 the World Cup was stolen while on display in London, and later unearthed by a dog, Pickles, who was out for a walk.

•

1974 Princess Anne escaped a kidnap attempt in Pall Mall, London, in which four people were wounded.

•

1980 *Mi Amigo*, the ship from which the pirate station Radio Caroline broadcast, sank.

•

1993 Tim Parry, 12, and Johnathan Ball, 3, were killed when two bombs exploded in Warrington.

21 MARCH

1925 Austin Peay, governor of Tennessee, approved a statute forbidding the teaching of Darwin's theory of evolution in state schools.

•

1935 Persia was renamed Iran by Reza Shah Pahlavi.

•

1945 Lord Alfred Douglas, poet and lover of Oscar Wilde, died in Lancing, Sussex, aged 74.

•

1946 Aneurin Bevan announced proposals for a National Health Service.

•

1960 South African police fired on black demonstrators at Sharpeville, killing 69.

•

1963 London Underground demonstrated its first driverless trains.

•

1963 Alcatraz maximum-security prison, California, was closed.

•

2006 the social media site Twitter was #founded.

1903 a drought caused Niagara Falls to run dry.

•

1933 Dachau concentration camp opened, its first prisoners being mostly communists and socialists.

•

1945 the Arab League was founded in Cairo.

•

1946 an Anglo-Transjordanian treaty ended the British mandate over what is now Jordan.

•

1993 the first Intel Pentium computer microprocessor, able to perform 100 million instructions a second, was released.

•

2002 a woman paralysed from the neck down, Miss B, won her legal right to die by having her treatment withdrawn.

23 MARCH

1801 Tsar Paul I was trampled to death in his bedroom by disgruntled officers.

•

1861 London's first trams began operating from Bayswater.

•

1919 Benito Mussolini formed the movement that two years later would become the Italian Fascist Party.

•

1966 the Archbishop of Canterbury, Michael Ramsey, visited Pope Paul VI in Rome for the first meeting in 400 years between leaders of the two churches.

•

1983 President Ronald Reagan announced plans for a space-based defence system later called Star Wars.

•

2001 the *Mir* space station broke up in the atmosphere before falling into the Pacific near Fiji.

24 MARCH

1603 King James VI of Scotland became James I of England on the death of Queen Elizabeth I.

•

1877 the Oxford and Cambridge boat race ended in the only dead heat of its history.

•

1944 German troops massacred 335 prisoners at the Ardeatine caves in Rome in revenge for a partisan attack.

•

1944 Allied airmen prepared to crawl through tunnels out of the German prison camp Stalag Luft III, in what became known as the Great Escape.

•

1958 Elvis Presley joined the US army.

•

1989 the tanker *Exxon Valdez* ran aground off Alaska, spilling crude oil into the sea.

25 MARCH

1199 King Richard I was wounded by a crossbow quarrel in France, and died 13 days later.

·

1752 Lady Day (commemorating the Annunciation of the Virgin Mary), ceased to be the legal beginning of the year in Britain.

·

1811 Percy Bysshe Shelley was sent down from University College, Oxford, for his authorship of a pamphlet entitled *The Necessity of Atheism*.

·

1924 Greece became a republic.

·

1957 the Treaty of Rome was signed, bringing into being the European Economic Community.

·

1996 the European Union banned the export of British beef because of fears of mad cow disease.

26 MARCH

1830 the Book of Mormon, a sacred text of the Church of Jesus Christ of Latter-day Saints, was published in America.

•

1885 in Woking, Surrey, Jeanette Pickersgill became the first person in modern times to be legally cremated in England.

•

1973 women were admitted to the London Stock Exchange for the first time.

•

1979 the American president Jimmy Carter witnessed the signing of a peace treaty by the Israeli prime minister Menachem Begin and the Egyptian president Anwar Sadat.

•

1981 Roy Jenkins, David Owen, William Rodgers and Shirley Williams launched the Social Democratic Party.

1871 the first international rugby match ended in a win for Scotland against England.

•

1915 Typhoid Mary (Mary Mallon), an Irish cook identified as an asymptomatic carrier of typhoid, was quarantined for life in New York.

•

1945 the last V-2 rockets launched by the Nazis fell on Orpington, Kent.

•

1958 Nikita Khrushchev became Soviet premier.

•

1963 the Beeching report listed 2,000 railway stations that could be closed.

•

1977 two jumbo jets collided on a runway in Tenerife, killing 560 people.

•

1980 a platform on the Alexander Kielland oil rig collapsed in the North Sea, killing 123 workers.

28 MARCH

1854 Britain and France declared war on Russia, the start of the Crimean War.

•

1930 Constantinople changed its name to Istanbul.

•

1939 Franco's Nationalist forces entered Madrid after a siege of three years.

•

1941 Virginia Woolf, novelist and critic, committed suicide in Rodmell, Sussex, aged 59.

•

1959 China dissolved the government of Tibet.

•

1964 the Great Train Robbers were sentenced to a total of 307 years' imprisonment.

•

2000 Anthony Powell, novelist (*A Dance to the Music of Time*), died near Frome, Somerset, aged 94.

29 MARCH

1827 Beethoven was buried in Vienna.

•

1867 the British North America Act was signed
by Queen Victoria.

•

1912 Captain Robert Scott, trapped in a tent near the
South Pole, made the last entry in his diary before he died.

•

1973 the last US troops left Vietnam, the conflict
having claimed the lives of 58,000 Americans and
2 million Vietnamese.

•

1981 the first London Marathon was held.

•

1992 US presidential candidate Bill Clinton said
he had smoked marijuana but had not inhaled.

1842 ether was used as an anaesthetic for the first time, by Dr Crawford Long.

•

1856 the Treaty of Paris ended the Crimean War.

•

1867 the USA purchased Alaska from Russia for $7.2 million (less than 2 cents an acre).

•

1979 Airey Neave, the Conservative Northern Ireland spokesman, was killed by a terrorist bomb in the House of Commons car park.

•

1981 President Reagan survived an assassination attempt, the bullet being removed from his lung.

•

1987 *Sunflowers*, by Vincent van Gogh, was sold at auction in London by Christie's for £24.75 million.

•

2002 the Queen Mother died aged 101.

31 MARCH

1889 Alexandre Gustave Eiffel's 984ft tower in Paris was officially opened.

•

1917 the US bought the 50 islands of the Danish West Indies and renamed them the Virgin Islands.

•

1920 the Church in Wales ceased to be part of the Church of England.

•

1959 the Dalai Lama fled Chinese repression after an uprising in Tibet and was granted asylum in India.

•

1966 the Labour Party under Harold Wilson swept to victory with a majority of 98 seats.

•

1990 protests by 100,000 people against the poll tax erupted into London's worst riots for a century.

1 APRIL

1875 *The Times* became the first British newspaper
to publish a daily weather chart.

•

1908 Britain's Territorial Army was formed.

•

1918 the RAF was founded, absorbing the Royal Flying
Corps and the Royal Naval Air Service.

•

1957 the BBC fooled the nation with a spoof documentary
about spaghetti crops in Switzerland.

•

1960 the US launched the first weather satellite.

•

1999 a legally binding minimum wage of £3.60 an hour
was introduced.

2 APRIL

1725 Giacomo Casanova, author and famed lover, was born in Venice.

•

1801 during the Battle of Copenhagen, Vice-Admiral Lord Nelson put his spyglass to his blind eye the better to ignore an order commanding him to disengage from combat.

•

1819 in Venice, Lord Byron met the 19-year-old Countess Teresa Guiccioli who would become his last love.

•

1836 Charles Dickens married Catherine Hogarth at St Luke's Church, Chelsea.

•

1948 Stalin's stringent control of traffic entering the city gave rise to the Berlin airlift.

•

1977 Red Rum won his third Grand National.

•

2005 Pope John Paul II died aged 84.

3 APRIL

1721 Sir Robert Walpole was appointed first lord of the Treasury and chancellor of the exchequer, effectively making him Britain's first prime minister.

•

1922 Stalin was appointed general secretary of the Soviet Communist Party.

•

1948 President Truman signed the Economic Assistance Act, putting into effect the Marshall Plan to support 16 countries in war-torn Europe.

•

1987 jewellery belonging to the Duchess of Windsor sold for £31 million, six times the estimated sum.

•

1993 the Grand National was declared void after a series of chaotic events at the start.

•

2010 the first Apple iPad was released.

4 APRIL

1687 King James II issued a declaration of indulgence permitting worship to take place outside the established Church of England.

•

1860 Billy Hamilton became the first eastbound Pony Express rider.

•

1930 Ras Tafari became Emperor Haile Selassie of Abyssinia.

•

1949 12 nations signed the North Atlantic Treaty for defence against Soviet aggression.

•

1958 the CND symbol was displayed for the first time.

•

1964 the Beatles occupied the top five places in the Billboard Hot 100.

•

1968 Martin Luther King Jr was assassinated in Memphis, Tennessee, aged 39.

•

1984 women from the peace camp at Greenham Common were evicted.

5 APRIL

1874 Johann Strauss's opera *Die Fledermaus* received its premiere in Vienna.

•

1951 Julius and Ethel Rosenberg were sentenced to death in the US for passing secrets to the Russians.

•

1955 Sir Winston Churchill resigned as prime minister, aged 80, because of failing health.

•

1976 Howard Hughes, one of the world's richest, and most reclusive, people, died on an aircraft in Houston aged 70.

•

1982 a British Task Force set sail for the Falkland Islands after the invasion by Argentina.

•

1997 the 150th Grand National was postponed for two days after an IRA bomb alert.

6 APRIL

1804 the High Possil meteorite landed in a quarry
on the outskirts of Glasgow.

•

1895 Oscar Wilde was arrested for gross indecency after
losing a libel case against the Marquess of Queensberry.

•

1896 the first modern Olympic Games began in Athens.

•

1917 the US declared war on Germany.

•

1974 Abba won the Eurovision Song Contest,
held in Brighton, with the song *Waterloo*.

•

1989 the government announced it was to abolish laws
guaranteeing jobs for life for dockers.

•

1999 two Libyans suspected of the 1988 Lockerbie bombing
were taken into custody in the Netherlands pending trial.

1141 Matilda, daughter of King Henry I, became the first woman ruler of England, though she was never crowned.

•

1827 John Walker, a Stockton-on-Tees chemist, sold the first of the friction matches he had invented.

•

1939 Mussolini invaded Albania.

•

1958 CND supporters marched from London to Aldermaston in their first ban-the-bomb protest.

•

1968 motor racing champion Jim Clark was killed in a race at Hockenheim.

•

1984 the South African runner Zola Budd, 17, was granted British citizenship after only a few weeks in the UK, provoking controversy.

•

1994 the Rwandan genocide began with massacres of Tutsis in Kigali.

8 APRIL

1838 Isambard Kingdom Brunel's steamship, the
Great Western, left Bristol for New York, the first
transatlantic crossing by a steam vessel.

•

1908 it was announced that Herbert Henry Asquith
would succeed Sir Henry Campbell-Bannerman
as prime minister.

•

1953 Jomo Kenyatta, later the first president of Kenya, was
sentenced to seven years' hard labour for his involvement
with the Mau-Mau uprising.

•

1973 the artist Pablo Picasso died near Cannes, France.

•

1986 Clint Eastwood won 72 per cent of the vote to become
mayor of Carmel, California.

•

1994 Kurt Cobain, singer with the group Nirvana, killed
himself, aged 27.

9 APRIL

1838 the National Gallery opened in Trafalgar Square, London.

•

1865 signalling that the American Civil War was all but over, General Robert E Lee surrendered the Confederate army of Northern Virginia to General Ulysses S Grant at Appomattox courthouse, Virginia.

•

1951 the first pay-per-view television was demonstrated in Chicago, Illinois, with three films costing $1 each to decode.

•

1969 Sikh bus drivers in Wolverhampton won the right to wear turbans on duty.

•

2003 Saddam Hussein's government was ousted from power in Iraq.

•

2005 the Prince of Wales married Camilla Parker Bowles in a civil ceremony.

1820 the first shipload of British settlers arrived
in South Africa.

•

1849 the safety pin was patented by Walter Hunt
of New York so that he could pay off a $15 debt.

•

1912 RMS *Titanic* set sail from Southampton on her
maiden voyage.

•

1925 F Scott Fitzgerald's *The Great Gatsby* was published.

•

1970 Paul McCartney announced he was leaving the Beatles.

•

1972 an earthquake in southern Iran killed more than
4,000 people.

•

1998 Northern Ireland peace talks ended with the signing
of the Good Friday Agreement.

1689 King William III and Queen Mary II were crowned
as joint monarchs.

•

1945 US troops liberated Buchenwald concentration camp.

•

1951 the Stone of Scone, upon which Scotland's sovereigns
traditionally sat when being crowned, was found after being
stolen by students.

•

1961 Adolf Eichmann went to trial in Jerusalem for his role
in the Holocaust.

•

1979 Idi Amin, the Ugandan dictator, fled to Libya
as Tanzanian forces closed in on Kampala.

•

1981 after a black man was arrested, hundreds of youths
rioted in Brixton, south London, leading to almost
400 injuries.

12 APRIL

1204 soldiers of the Fourth Crusade sacked Constantinople.

•

1606 a union flag incorporating the St George's cross of England and the St Andrew's cross of Scotland was introduced by King James I.

•

1945 President Franklin D Roosevelt died in office, 11 weeks into his fourth term, and was succeeded by Harry Truman.

•

1955 US physician Dr Jonas Salk's polio vaccine was pronounced safe, effective and potent.

•

1961 Yuri Gagarin became the first man to be sent into orbital space flight, circling the earth in 1hr 48min.

•

1981 the first Space Shuttle mission began when *Columbia* took off.

13 APRIL

1742 Handel's *Messiah* received its world premiere in Dublin.

•

1829 King George IV gave the royal assent to the Catholic Emancipation Act, allowing Catholics to become MPs.

•

1919 hundreds of Indian nationalists were killed when British troops opened fire on a crowd in Amritsar.

•

1964 Sidney Poitier became the first black actor to win the best actor Oscar, for *Lilies of the Field*.

•

1970 *Apollo 13* astronaut Jack Swigert heard an oxygen tank explode and uttered the memorable phrase: "Okay Houston, we've had a problem here".

•

1992 Neil Kinnock resigned as Labour leader after losing the election.

1865 President Abraham Lincoln was shot by John Wilkes Booth at Ford's Theatre, Washington DC, and died the next day.

•

1869 John Van Heusen, creator of shirts with integral collars, was born in Albany, New York.

•

1894 Edison's kinetoscope (moving pictures) was shown in a public booth for the first time.

•

1931 the Highway Code was first issued.

•

1942 Malta received the George Cross for its defiance of the Axis forces.

•

1988 Mikhail Gorbachev announced the phased withdrawal of Soviet troops from Afghanistan.

•

2014 276 schoolgirls were abducted in Nigeria by the Boko Haram terror group.

15 APRIL

1755 Samuel Johnson's *Dictionary of the English Language* was published.

•

1770 the chemist Joseph Priestley discovered india rubber could rub out lead pencil marks.

•

1802 Dorothy Wordsworth recorded in her diary a walk with her brother William, on which she "never saw daffodils so beautiful".

•

1912 the White Star liner *Titanic* struck an iceberg and sank with the loss of more than 1,500 lives.

•

1945 British troops entered the Bergen-Belsen concentration camp.

•

1955 Ray Kroc, founder of McDonald's, opened his first drive-in restaurant in Des Plaines, Illinois.

•

1989 96 football fans were crushed at the Hillsborough ground, Sheffield.

1746 the Battle of Culloden, the last battle on British soil, was fought.

•

1943 the Swiss chemist Albert Hofmann accidentally discovered the hallucinogenic drug LSD after experimenting with ergot.

•

1947 the phrase "Cold War" was coined in a speech delivered by the US statesman Bernard Baruch.

•

1953 the Royal Yacht *Britannia* was launched.

•

1964 12 men were given jail sentences totalling 307 years for their part in the Great Train Robbery.

•

1993 the UN security council created a safe haven for Bosnian Muslims under siege in the town of Srebrenica.

17 APRIL

1397 Geoffrey Chaucer read *The Canterbury Tales* for the first time at the court of King Richard II.

•

1941 Yugoslavia surrendered to Germany.

•

1951 The Peak District became the first national park in Britain.

•

1961 1,500 CIA-trained exiles landed in the Bay of Pigs, Cuba, to try to ignite a rebellion against Castro.

•

1969 Bernadette Devlin, 22, won the seat of Mid-Ulster and became the youngest female MP.

•

1984 WPC Yvonne Fletcher was shot dead outside the Libyan embassy in London.

•

1986 the British journalist John McCarthy was kidnapped in Beirut.

18 APRIL

1593 Shakespeare's first published work, the poem
Venus and Adonis, was entered into the Stationers' Register.

•

1775 at the start of the American War of Independence,
Paul Revere rode to give warning of the arrival of British
troops.

•

1906 San Francisco was struck by an earthquake that
was responsible for an estimated 3,000 deaths.

•

1949 Eire became the Republic of Ireland, ceasing to be part
of the British Commonwealth.

•

1955 Albert Einstein, physicist, died — research showed
the part of his brain responsible for mathematical thought
was 15 per cent wider than average.

•

1980 Britain's last African colony Rhodesia gained
independence as Zimbabwe.

1521 Martin Luther ended his defence at the Diet of Worms with: I cannot and will not recant anything. God help me. Amen.

•

1927 the actress Mae West was convicted of obscenity for writing, producing and directing a Broadway musical called *Sex*.

•

1943 the Warsaw ghetto uprising began.

•

1956 Prince Rainier of Monaco married the American actress Grace Kelly.

•

1993 a siege near Waco, Texas, ended with the deaths of 76 members of the Branch Davidians including David Koresh.

•

1995 168 people died in Timothy McVeigh's bombing of an Oklahoma City government building.

1653 Oliver Cromwell dissolved the Rump Parliament, the small body of MPs that remained after the 1648 purge of the Long Parliament.

•

1859 Charles Dickens's *A Tale of Two Cities* was published.

•

1945 Hitler spent his final birthday in his Berlin bunker while Soviet troops were at the gates of the city.

•

1968 Enoch Powell made his Rivers of Blood speech against rising immigration.

•

1981 Steve Davis won his first World Snooker Championship at 23 years old.

•

1999 teenagers Eric Harris and Dylan Klebold killed 12 students and a teacher at Columbine High School, Colorado.

753 BC the city of Rome is said to have been founded
by Romulus.

•

1916 Sir Roger Casement was arrested for high treason
for his role in plotting the Easter Rising in Dublin.

•

1918 German air ace Manfred von Richthofen,
the Red Baron, was killed.

•

1945 Russian troops entered Berlin.

•

1955 national newspapers were published for the
first time in nearly a month after a strike by maintenance
workers ended.

•

1960 Brasília became the capital of Brazil.

•

1983 £1 coins replaced paper banknotes in Britain.

•

1989 Chinese students demanding democratic reform
poured into Tiananmen Square, Beijing.

1838 the British packet steamer *Sirius* made the first transatlantic crossing by steam power alone, reaching New York from Cork in 18 days and 10 hours.

·

1969 Robin Knox-Johnston sailed into Falmouth harbour, winning a race for non-stop, single-handed circumnavigation of the globe.

·

1971 Haitian dictator Francois "Papa Doc" Duvalier died after ruling for 14 years.

·

1972 an IRA bomb killed six people at Aldershot barracks.

·

1984 Britain broke off diplomatic relations with Libya after the fatal shooting of WPC Yvonne Fletcher.

·

1993 Stephen Lawrence was murdered at a bus stop in Eltham, London, aged 18.

23 APRIL

1927 the BBC made its first live radio broadcast of the FA Cup final from Wembley, where Cardiff City beat Arsenal, the only time the tournament has been won by a Welsh side.

•

1968 the first decimal coins (five and ten pence pieces) appeared in Britain, ahead of full introduction three years later.

•

1979 a teacher was killed during the Southall race riots.

•

1984 it was announced that the virus that caused Aids had been isolated.

•

1985 Coca-Cola changed its formula, but the reaction to New Coke quickly forced the company to offer the original taste once more.

24 APRIL

1558 Mary Queen of Scots married the French Dauphin François at Notre Dame, Paris.

•

1916 the Easter Rising began in Dublin, with rebels against British rule proclaiming an Irish Republic.

•

1957 *The Sky At Night* was first broadcast on BBC television.

•

1967 Russian cosmonaut Vladimir Komarov became the first person killed on a space mission when the parachute of *Soyuz 1* failed to deploy.

•

1990 the space shuttle *Discovery* was launched, carrying the Hubble space telescope.

•

1993 an IRA bomb at Bishopsgate in the City of London killed a *News of the World* photographer and injured 40 other people.

1816 the poet Lord Byron left England, never to return.

•

1856 Charles Lutwidge Dodgson, who wrote under the name of Lewis Carroll, met Alice Liddell, the inspiration for his Alice books.

•

1859 work began on the Suez Canal.

•

1953 Francis Crick and James Watson revealed the role of DNA in human biology.

•

1956 *Heartbreak Hotel* became Elvis Presley's first American chart-topper.

•

1980 eight soldiers were killed in a failed US bid to rescue hostages in Teheran.

•

1983 the first instalment of the so-called *Hitler Diaries*, said to be written by the Fuhrer, was published in Germany.

26 APRIL

1336 Italian poet and scholar Francesco Petrarca (Petrarch) climbed Mont Ventoux, in France, for pleasure, the first recorded occurrence of tourism.

•

1915 Australian and New Zealand forces landed at Gallipoli.

•

1923 Prince Albert, Duke of York, the future George VI, married Lady Elizabeth Bowes Lyon.

•

1937 German aircraft destroyed the Basque city of Guernica.

•

1986 a reactor exploded at the Chernobyl nuclear plant in Ukraine.

•

1992 worshippers celebrated the Russian Orthodox Easter in Moscow for the first time in 74 years.

•

1994 voting began in South Africa's first all-race elections, resulting in Nelson Mandela's presidency.

27 APRIL

1773 the British government passed the Tea Act, removing duties on tea shipped to America by the East India Company and leading indirectly to the Boston Tea Party.

•

1828 the London Zoological Gardens opened in Regent's Park.

•

1940 Heinrich Himmler ordered the construction of Auschwitz.

•

1941 German troops marched into Athens, and erected a swastika flag on the Acropolis.

•

1945 Russian and American troops joined hands at the River Elbe in Germany.

•

1968 the Abortion Act, presented by David Steel, came into force.

•

1992 Betty Boothroyd was elected the first female Speaker of the House of Commons.

28 APRIL

1789 the crew of HMS *Bounty* mutinied against the harsh regime of Captain Bligh.

•

1945 Benito Mussolini was killed by Italian partisans.

•

1947 Thor Heyerdahl and five crewmates set sail from Peru on the *Kon-Tiki* raft to prove that Peruvians could have colonised Polynesia.

•

1953 Japan regained the right to self-government, lost at the end of the Second World War.

•

1969 General Charles de Gaulle resigned as president of France after 11 years.

•

1996 Martin Bryant shot dead 35 people in the Port Arthur massacre in Tasmania.

1429 Joan of Arc entered Orleans, relieving its siege by the English.

•

1770 Captain Cook landed in Australia, naming the continent New South Wales.

•

1862 Union forces under David Farragut capture New Orleans during the American Civil War.

•

1913 Gideon Sundback patented an improved zip.

•

1916 a 9,000-strong British force surrendered to the Turks after having been besieged for 143 days in Kut-el-Amara (modern Iraq).

•

1945 Adolf Hitler married Eva Braun in his Berlin bunker.

•

1945 US forces liberated Dachau concentration camp.

•

1967 Muhammad Ali is stripped of his heavyweight title for refusing to serve in the US army.

•

2011 Prince William married Catherine Middleton at Westminster Abbey.

30 APRIL

311 the Roman Emperor Galerius published an
edict permitting Christians to practise their religion
without persecution.

•

1665 Samuel Pepys made his first diary reference to the
great plague.

•

1789 George Washington was inaugurated as the first
American president.

•

1803 the US government bought Louisiana from
the French for $15 million.

•

1973 President Nixon accepted responsibility for bugging
at the Watergate complex.

•

1975 Saigon fell to the Vietcong and was renamed
Ho Chi Minh City.

•

1980 terrorists seized the Iranian embassy in London.

•

1993 the tennis player Monica Seles was stabbed during
a match in Hamburg.

1661 there was dancing around a 40m (130ft) high maypole, the tallest in London.

•

1707 the union of England and Scotland was proclaimed.

•

1851 the Great Exhibition at Hyde Park was opened by Queen Victoria.

•

1869 the Folies Bergère music hall opened in Paris.

•

1931 President Hoover opened the 102-storey Empire State Building.

•

1945 Germany announced the death of Hitler.

•

1961 Fidel Castro, prime minister of Cuba, declared the country a socialist nation and abolished elections.

•

1994 racing driver Ayrton Senna was killed while leading the San Marino Grand Prix, at Imola.

2 MAY

1536 Anne Boleyn, charged with incest and adultery, was taken to the Tower of London.

•

1887 the first US patent for celluloid film was submitted and in 1902 the 14-minute-long *Le Voyage dans la Lune* had its premiere.

•

1966 *The Times* devoted its front page to advertising for the last time.

•

1982 during the Falklands conflict, the Argentine cruiser *General Belgrano* was sunk by the British submarine *Conqueror*.

•

1997 the Labour leader Tony Blair was elected prime minister.

•

2011 Osama bin Laden was killed in a covert operation by US special forces in Pakistan.

1494 Columbus discovered Jamaica.

•

1621 the lord chancellor, Sir Francis Bacon, was charged with accepting bribes to grant monopoly patents, and impeached.

•

1788 *The Star and Evening Advertiser,* London's first daily evening newspaper, was published.

•

1945 Rangoon, the capital of Burma, was captured from the Japanese by British forces under Lord Mountbatten.

•

1951 King George VI and Queen Elizabeth formally opened the Festival of Britain.

•

1968 surgeons performed the first heart transplant in Britain.

•

1986 a bomb killed 21 people at Colombo airport, Sri Lanka.

1904 America took over the construction of the
Panama Canal.

•

1926 the General Strike started.

•

1932 the American gangster Al Capone went to prison
for tax evasion.

•

1970 four Kent State University students were shot dead
by the National Guard during demonstrations against
the Vietnam War.

•

1979 Margaret Thatcher became Britain's first female
prime minister.

•

1982 an Argentine missile sank HMS *Sheffield* during
the Falklands conflict.

•

2000 Ken Livingstone was elected first Mayor of London
as an independent candidate after being expelled from
the Labour Party.

1260 Kublai Khan became ruler of the Mongol empire.

•

1821 Napoleon died in exile on St Helena.

•

1881 Louis Pasteur tested his inoculations against anthrax upon an ox, several cows and 25 sheep.

•

1905 fingerprint evidence was used for the first time in Britain to secure a murder conviction.

•

1980 the siege of the Iranian embassy in London ended when SAS soldiers stormed the building.

•

1981 having refused food for 66 days, the hunger striker Bobby Sands died in the Maze prison in Northern Ireland, aged 27.

•

2005 Tony Blair secured a third term in government for Labour.

6 MAY

1840 the first adhesive postage stamp, the Penny Black, went into use.

•

1882 Lord Frederick Cavendish, the British secretary for Ireland, and his undersecretary TH Burke, were murdered by Fenians in Dublin.

•

1889 the Prince of Wales opened the Eiffel Tower in Paris.

•

1937 the German airship *Hindenberg* exploded on landing in New Jersey, USA, killing 36 of those on board.

•

1954 Roger Bannister became the first man to run a mile in less than four minutes.

•

1966 Ian Brady and Myra Hindley, the Moors murderers, were jailed for life.

•

1994 the Channel Tunnel was officially opened.

1663 the first of a series of playhouses known as the
Theatre Royal was opened in Drury Lane, London.

•

1765 HMS *Victory*, which was to be Nelson's flagship
at the Battle of Trafalgar in 1805, was launched
at Chatham Dockyard.

•

1915 1,198 people perished when the British transatlantic
liner *Lusitania* was torpedoed by a German submarine
off the Irish coast.

•

1945 General Alfred Jodl signed Germany's surrender
to the Allies (effective from May 8), near Reims in France.

•

1959 an agreement was reached enabling Britain to buy
components of atomic weapons (other than nuclear
warheads) from the US.

8 MAY

1660 the monarchy was restored and Charles II proclaimed king.

•

1790 France began to go metric when its National Assembly approved Talleyrand's proposal for a unified system of weights and measures.

•

1945 VE (Victory in Europe) Day was celebrated throughout Britain (with the exception of the Channel Islands, liberated the following day).

•

1961 the House of Commons refused to allow Tony Benn, who had inherited a viscountcy, to take up the Bristol South East seat he had retained in a by-election.

•

1987 eight IRA men and a civilian were killed by an SAS ambush in Loughgall, Co Armagh.

9 MAY

1671 Irish adventurer Thomas Blood attempted to steal the Crown Jewels from the Tower of London.

•

1918 Lytton Strachey's new-style biography, *Eminent Victorians*, was published.

•

1945 Jersey and Guernsey were liberated from German occupation.

•

1946 King Victor Emanuel of Italy abdicated and was briefly succeeded by his son Umberto II.

•

1949 Britain's first launderette opened in Queensway, London.

•

1955 West Germany was accepted into Nato.

•

1960 Enovid became the first approved oral contraceptive pill.

•

1972 Israeli commandos stormed a hijacked passenger plane in Tel Aviv and released the 100 people held hostage.

10 MAY

1857 the Indian Mutiny began.

•

1869 the Central Pacific and Union Pacific railroads met at Promontory Summit, Utah, completing America's first transcontinental railway.

•

1922 Dr Ivy Williams became the first woman to be called to the English Bar.

•

1940 Winston Churchill succeeded Neville Chamberlain as prime minister.

•

1941 Rudolf Hess, deputy leader of the Nazi Party, parachuted into Scotland in an apparent attempt to negotiate a peace deal, but was arrested and imprisoned.

•

1967 Mick Jagger and Keith Richards, of the Rolling Stones, appeared before magistrates on drugs charges.

330 Constantinople became the capital of the
Roman Empire.

•

1626 Peter Minuit, governor of the Dutch colony of
New Netherland, authorised the purchase of Manhattan
from local Native Americans.

•

1818 the Old Vic theatre in London opened as the
Royal Coburg theatre.

•

1985 56 people were killed and more than 200 injured
when fire broke out at Bradford City football ground.

•

1998 India carried out nuclear tests, provoking tension
with Pakistan.

•

1998 the first euro coin was minted in France.

•

2000 India welcomed its billionth citizen when a girl
was born at Safdarjung Hospital in Delhi.

12 MAY

1935 a chance meeting took place between two alcoholics, Dr Robert Smith and William Wilson, which led to the founding of Alcoholics Anonymous.

•

1967 Stansted was approved to become London's third international airport.

•

1971 Mick Jagger married Bianca Perez Morena de Macias despite a row with journalists which threatened to end the proceedings.

1981 Francis Hughes, the second IRA member to starve to death on a hunger strike campaigning for political status for IRA prisoners, died in the Maze Prison, near Belfast.

•

1994 the Labour Party leader John Smith died of a heart attack, aged 55.

13 MAY

1568 a confederacy of Scottish Protestants defeated the forces of Mary Queen of Scots at the Battle of Langside, near Glasgow, and Mary fled to England.

•

1607 the first permanent English settlement in America was established at Jamestown, Virginia.

•

1940 the novelist and travel writer Bruce Chatwin was born.

•

1943 General Alexander announced the surrender of Italian and German forces in Tunisia.

•

1981 Pope John Paul II survived an assassination attempt by a Turkish gunman in St Peter's Square, Rome.

•

1995 the 33-year-old Scottish mountaineer Alison Hargreaves became the first woman to climb Everest without supplemental oxygen.

14 MAY

1264 the English barons under Simon de Montford defeated King Henry III at the battle of Lewes.

·

1796 the British physician Edward Jenner carried out the first successful vaccination against smallpox.

·

1842 *The Illustrated London News* was published for the first time.

·

1939 a Peruvian girl, Lina Medina, became the youngest known mother when giving birth, aged five, to a son.

·

1955 the Warsaw Pact was signed by the Soviet Union, Albania, Bulgaria, Czechoslovakia, East Germany, Hungary, Poland and Romania.

·

1991 Winnie Mandela was sentenced to six years' imprisonment for complicity in the kidnapping and beating of four youths.

1718 the machine gun was patented by James Puckle, a London lawyer.

•

1800 shots were fired at King George III in the royal box of the Drury Lane Theatre, London.

•

1928 Mickey Mouse made his first appearance, in the Disney cartoon *Plane Crazy*.

•

1928 the Australian Flying Doctor service began.

•

1936 Amy Johnson arrived in England after a record-breaking flight from South Africa.

•

1941 the first Allied jet plane, the Gloster-Whittle E28/39, made its maiden flight.

•

1957 Britain's first H-bomb exploded over Malden Island in the Pacific.

•

1991 Edith Cresson became France's first woman prime minister.

16 MAY

1717 Voltaire was imprisoned in the Bastille after his satirical poem *La Henriade* riled the French administration.

•

1770 aged 15, the Dauphin (later Louis XVI) married the 14-year-old Marie Antoinette.

•

1920 Joan of Arc was canonised in Rome by Pope Benedict XV.

•

1929 the first Academy Awards were presented in Los Angeles.

•

1943 the Warsaw Ghetto uprising ended.

•

1991 the Queen, on a tour of the US, became the first British monarch to address a joint meeting of Congress.

•

1997 Mobutu Sese Seko, dictator of Zaire for 32 years, fled the country.

17 MAY

1792 24 merchants meeting in Wall Street founded the New York Stock Exchange.

•

1875 the first Kentucky Derby was run at Louisville and won by Aristides.

•

1900 the British garrison in Mafeking, Cape Colony, was relieved after a 217-day siege.

•

1916 the Daylight Saving Act was passed in Britain, giving rise to much confusion when clocks went forward four days later.

•

1943 the Dambuster raid took place as bouncing bombs, the invention of Sir Barnes Wallis, were dropped on dams in the Ruhr valley.

•

1969 the Russian craft *Venera 5* landed on Venus.

18 MAY

1291 Acre, the remaining Christian stronghold in the Holy Land, fell to the Saracens.

•

1804 Napoleon Bonaparte was proclaimed Emperor of France.

•

1910 the Earth passed through the tail of Halley's Comet, prompting predictions of plague, tidal waves and disaster.

•

1944 Monte Cassino was taken by Polish troops.

•

1953 test pilot Jackie Cochran became the first woman to break the sound barrier, flying at 1050kmh (652.5mph).

•

1980 after a month of tremors, Mount St Helens volcano in Washington State erupted, killing 57 people and sending a volcanic plume 60,000ft into the air.

1536 Anne Boleyn was beheaded.

•

1802 Napoleon founded the Legion of Honour.

•

1897 Oscar Wilde was released from Reading Gaol.

•

1900 Britain annexed the Tonga Islands in the
South Pacific.

•

1906 the Simplon Tunnel, linking Italy and Switzerland
through the Alps, was officially opened.

•

1935 TE Lawrence (Lawrence of Arabia) was killed
in a motorcycle accident.

•

1962 Marilyn Monroe sang *Happy Birthday* at a celebration
for President John F Kennedy at Madison Square Garden,
New York.

•

1974 Valéry Giscard d'Estaing was elected as the president
of France.

20 MAY

325 the Catholic Church's first ecumenical council met in Nicaea (modern Iznik, Turkey).

•

1608 Shakespeare's *Antony and Cleopatra* was entered in the Stationers' Register.

•

1873 Levi Strauss received a patent for blue jeans.

•

1927 Charles Lindbergh Jr took off from Long Island on what was to be the first transatlantic solo flight.

•

1932 Amelia Earhart took off from Harbor Grace, Newfoundland, on what would be the first transatlantic solo flight by a woman.

•

1941 German paratroops began their invasion of Crete.

•

1977 the original Orient Express began its last journey from Paris to Istanbul.

1840 Captain William Hobson proclaimed New Zealand to be a British colony.

·

1894 Queen Victoria opened the Manchester Ship Canal.

·

1904 Fifa, the Fédération Internationale de Football Association, was established.

·

1916 daylight saving was introduced, with the clocks going forward one hour.

·

1927 Charles Lindbergh Jr arrived in Paris after flying from New York in a little over 33 hours.

·

1932 Amelia Earhart landed in Ireland to become the first woman to fly the Atlantic solo.

·

1979 Elton John became the first western rock star to perform in the Soviet Union.

1455 the Yorkists won the first Battle of St Albans, taking the Lancastrian King Henry VI prisoner.

•

1897 the Prince of Wales opened the Blackwall Tunnel under the Thames in London.

•

1906 a patent was granted to Wilbur and Orville Wright for flying machines.

•

1958 Mao Zedong started the Great Leap Forward in China.

•

1970 the tour of England by South Africa's cricket team was called off.

•

1972 Ceylon adopted a new constitution, and changed its name to Sri Lanka.

•

1981 Peter Sutcliffe, the Yorkshire Ripper, was sentenced to life imprisonment.

23 MAY

1618 the second Defenestration of Prague took place, leading to the Thirty Years War.

·

1785 Benjamin Franklin announced his invention of bifocals.

·

1934 Bonnie (Parker) and Clyde (Barrow), outlaws, were killed in an ambush near Gibland, Louisiana.

·

1937 John D Rockefeller, tycoon and philanthropist, died in Florida.

·

1977 more than 100 children were taken hostage near Assen in the Netherlands in a protest by South Moluccans.

·

1984 nine people died during a tour of the Abbeystead water treatment plant near Lancaster following a build-up of methane gas (and seven others died later of their injuries).

24 MAY

1809 Dartmoor prison opened, to house French PoWs.

·

1844 Samuel Morse sent the first telegraph:
What hath God wrought?

·

1930 Amy Johnson became the first woman to fly solo
from England to Australia.

·

1940 Igor Sikorksy made his inaugural flight in what
became the world's first mass-produced helicopter.

·

1941 HMS *Hood* was sunk by the *Bismarck* off Greenland.

·

1956 Swiss singer Lys Assia won the first Eurovision
Song Contest, held in Lugano, Switzerland.

·

1976 the London to Washington Concorde service began.

·

2001 23 people were killed at a wedding party in Jerusalem
after the dance floor collapsed.

1660 King Charles II landed at Dover after nine years in exile.

•

1787 the Philadelphia Convention met to draw up the US Constitution.

•

1833 the first flower show in Britain was held by the Royal Horticultural Society in Chiswick, west London.

•

1935 the American athlete Jesse Owens set or equalled six world records in less than one hour.

•

1951 Guy Burgess and Donald Maclean, British Foreign Office officials later discovered to have spied for Russia, disappeared from London.

•

1967 Celtic became the first British team to win football's European Cup, defeating Inter Milan.

•

1977 *Star Wars* was released.

26 MAY

1797 £1 and £2 banknotes were first issued in England.

•

1868 the last public execution in Britain took place in London, when Michael Barrett was hanged for the 1867 Clerkenwell bombing.

•

1897 Bram Stoker's *Dracula* was published.

•

1923 the first Le Mans 24-hour motor race was won by André Lagache and René Léonard, with an average speed of 57.2mph.

•

1940 the order was given to begin Operation Dynamo to evacuate troops from Dunkirk.

•

1950 the British government announced the end of petrol rationing.

•

1986 the European flag was adopted as the symbol of the European Community.

27 MAY

1679 parliament passed the Habeas Corpus Act, protecting citizens against false arrest and imprisonment.

•

1703 the Russian tsar Peter the Great proclaimed St Petersburg the nation's new capital.

•

1936 the liner RMS *Queen Mary* left Southampton on her maiden voyage to New York via Cherbourg.

•

1937 the Golden Gate Bridge in San Francisco was opened.

•

1941 the German battleship *Bismarck* was sunk, with the loss of 2,100 lives.

•

1942 Reinhard Heydrich was fatally wounded in an attack in Prague.

•

1993 a car bomb exploded outside the Uffizi Gallery in Florence, killing five people.

1588 the Spanish Armada set sail from Lisbon.

·

1742 Britain's first indoor swimming pool opened
in Goodman's Fields, London.

·

1959 Able and Baker, two monkeys, became the first
creatures to survive a flight in space.

·

1961 Amnesty International was founded in London.

·

1967 Sir Francis Chichester arrived in Plymouth after
sailing single-handed around the world in *Gipsy Moth IV*.

·

1982 British troops recaptured Port Darwin and Goose
Green during the Falklands conflict.

·

1987 Mathias Rust, a West German, exposed the inadequacy
of Soviet air defences by flying his Cessna into Red Square,
Moscow, from Helsinki.

29 MAY

1919 the mechanic Charles Strite, of Minnesota, filed
a patent for his pop-up toaster.

•

1953 Sir Edmund Hillary and Sherpa Tenzing Norgay
reached the summit of Mount Everest.

•

1974 Northern Ireland was brought under direct rule
from Westminster a day after the collapse of the Northern
Ireland executive.

•

1982 Pope Paul II, in the first papal visit to Britain since
1531, prayed alongside the Archbishop of Canterbury
in Canterbury Cathedral.

•

1985 41 spectators died at the Heysel Stadium in Belgium,
when riots broke out before the Liverpool v Juventus
European Cup Final.

1381 the Peasants' Revolt began.

•

1431 Joan of Arc was burned at the stake at Rouen
by the English.

•

1536 Jane Seymour became Henry VIII's third wife.

•

1593 Christopher Marlowe, dramatist and possible spy,
died in a brawl in Deptford aged 29.

•

1656 the Grenadier Guards were formed.

•

1688 Alexander Pope, poet and essayist, died at Twickenham
aged 56.

•

1842 John Francis attempted to assassinate Queen Victoria
as she rode in her carriage with Prince Albert along
Constitution Hill in London.

•

1942 Air Marshal Arthur (Bomber) Harris launched the first
thousand-bomber raid on Cologne.

1669 Samuel Pepys concluded his diary because of fears about his eyesight.

•

1859 the chimes of Big Ben in London rang for the first time.

•

1916 the Battle of Jutland, the only major sea battle of the First World War, began.

•

1927 after more than 15 million had been made, the last Ford Model T rolled off the production line.

•

1985 English teams were banned by the FA from playing in European competition following the Heysel stadium tragedy.

•

2008 a new 100m record of 9.72 seconds was set by Jamaican athlete Usain Bolt.

1 JUNE

1599 the Archbishop of Canterbury ordered a burning of so-called offensive books, including Marlowe's translation of *Ovid*.

•

1880 the first public telephone box went into service in the United States.

•

1939 the submarine HMS *Thetis* sank on her first dive off Liverpool with the loss of 99 lives.

•

1958 Charles de Gaulle became the last prime minister of France's Fourth Republic.

•

1962 Adolf Eichmann was hanged in Israel for his role in the Holocaust.

•

1994 South Africa rejoined the Commonwealth after 33 years.

•

2001 Crown Prince Dipendra massacred Nepal's royal family before shooting himself.

2 JUNE

597 St Augustine baptised King Ethelbert of Kent.

•

1162 Thomas à Becket was ordained, to be consecrated as Archbishop of Canterbury the next day.

•

1896 Guglielmo Marconi patented his wireless telegraphy apparatus.

•

1910 CS Rolls (FH Royce's business partner) became the first airman to fly a round trip over the Channel.

•

1946 Italy was proclaimed a republic.

•

1953 Queen Elizabeth II was crowned.

•

1979 John Paul II arrived in Poland, the first pope to visit a communist country.

•

1994 25 senior police, army and MI5 officers died when an RAF Chinook crashed on the Mull of Kintyre.

3 JUNE

1898 Samuel Plimsoll, MP who secured safety legislation requiring a load line to be painted on British merchant ships, died.

•

1937 the former Edward VIII married American divorcée Wallis Simpson.

•

1949 Wesley Anthony Brown became the first African-American to graduate from the US Naval Academy.

•

1956 third-class travel ceased on Britain's railways.

•

1962 an Air France Boeing 707, bound for Atlanta, Georgia, crashed at Orly airport, Paris, killing 130.

•

1989 the Chinese army moved tanks into Tiananmen Square, Beijing, to crush democracy protests.

•

2017 eight people were killed by terrorists in attacks around London Bridge.

4 JUNE

1728 King George III, reigned 1760–1820, was born at Norfolk House, St James's Square, London (later General Eisenhower's wartime headquarters).

•

1878 Turkey ceded Cyprus to Britain in return for the promise of military aid against the Russians.

•

1913 the suffragette Emily Davison was fatally injured when she ran in front of King George V's horse at the Epsom Derby.

•

1927 the US defeated Britain in the first official Ryder Cup golf tournament, in Worcester, Massachusetts.

•

1940 on the last day of the Allied evacuation from Dunkirk, Winston Churchill called the rescue operation a miracle of deliverance.

•

1944 Rome was taken by Allied forces.

•

1970 Tonga, a protected state since 1900, gained its independence from Britain.

5 JUNE

1661 Isaac Newton was admitted as a student to Trinity College, Cambridge.

•

1944 just before midnight, troops took off from airfields on their way to Normandy for D-Day.

•

1967 the Six Day War began when Israel made surprise air attacks in Egypt.

•

1972 the Duke of Windsor was buried at Frogmore, Windsor.

•

1975 the Suez Canal was reopened by Egypt after being closed since the Six Day War.

•

1975 the UK voted two-to-one in a referendum to stay in the EEC.

•

1977 one of the first personal computers, the Apple II, went on sale.

6 JUNE

1844 the YMCA was founded in London.

·

1907 Persil, the first household detergent, was launched in Germany.

·

1944 just after midnight, three Horsa gliders carrying British forces landed near Pegasus Bridge over the Caen Canal, Normandy, taken in the first exchange of fire of D-Day.

·

1962 the Beatles first met future producer George Martin at an Abbey Road audition.

·

1968 Robert Kennedy, US attorney-general (1961–64), died, the victim of an assassin, in Los Angeles, California.

·

1984 the Indian army opened fire on Sikh separatists in the Golden Temple in Amritsar, killing hundreds of people.

7 JUNE

1929 the Vatican City was established with the ratification of the Lateran Treaty by Italy.

•

1939 George VI became the first British monarch to visit the US.

•

1950 the first episode of *The Archers* was broadcast by the BBC.

•

1965 Sony introduced home videotape recorders with the Betamax system.

•

1967 Israeli troops entered Jerusalem during the Six Day War.

•

1973 Willy Brandt was the first West German leader to visit Israel.

•

1977 millions of Britons celebrated Queen Elizabeth II's Silver Jubilee with street parties.

•

1982 Graceland, Elvis Presley's former home in Memphis, Tennessee, was opened to the public.

8 JUNE

1374 Geoffrey Chaucer was appointed controller of customs for the Port of London.

•

1949 George Orwell's novel *Nineteen Eighty-Four* was published.

•

1953 the US Supreme Court ruled restaurants in the District of Columbia could not refuse to serve African-Americans.

•

1968 James Earl Ray, wanted for the murder of American civil rights leader Martin Luther King Jr, was arrested in London.

•

1972 in Vietnam, a photograph was taken of a nine-year old girl, Phan Thi Kim Phuc, being burned by napalm.

•

1986 Kurt Waldheim was elected president of Austria despite allegations he had been involved in Nazi atrocities.

9 JUNE

68 the Roman emperor Nero committed suicide.

•

1549 on Pentecost Sunday, the *Book of Common Prayer* was first used by the Church of England.

•

1904 the London Symphony Orchestra gave its inaugural concert.

•

1934 the cartoon character Donald Duck made his screen debut in *The Wise Little Hen.*

•

1969 General Franco closed Spain's frontier with Gibraltar.

•

1975 the House of Commons was broadcast live by radio for the first time.

•

1983 Margaret Thatcher won a second general election by a landslide, beating Michael Foot's Labour Party by 397 seats to 209.

10 JUNE

1190 leading an army to the Third Crusade, German emperor Frederick Barbarossa drowned in a river.

·

1692 the first of the men and women to be hanged after the Salem witch-hunt was executed.

·

1829 Oxford won the first Boat Race, at Henley-on-Thames.

·

1944 the Nazis massacred hundreds of French villagers in Oradour-sur-Glane, in retaliation for Resistance attacks.

·

1990 a British Airways aircraft landed safely at Southampton airport after a faulty windscreen led to the captain being partially sucked out of the cockpit.

·

2000 the new Millennium footbridge over the Thames was closed after users reported that it wobbled.

11 JUNE

1509 King Henry VIII married Catherine of Aragon.

•

1955 in an accident at the Le Mans race, at least 80 people were killed when a car exploded after hitting a bank of the track.

•

1959 the first experimental man-carrying hovercraft was launched at Cowes, Isle of Wight.

•

1962 Frank Morris and John and Clarence Anglin became the only prisoners to escape from Alcatraz.

•

1963 George C Wallace, Alabama's state governor, barred the path to James A Hood and Vivian J Malone, two black students attempting to enrol at the University of Alabama.

•

1987 Margaret Thatcher celebrated her third election victory.

12 JUNE

1897 Karl Elsener took out a patent for a penknife later known as the Swiss army knife.

•

1908 the Rotherhithe-Stepney road tunnel was opened under the Thames.

•

1942 on her 13th birthday, Anne Frank received a diary.

•

1964 Nelson Mandela was sentenced to life imprisonment for conspiring to overthrow the government by sabotage.

•

1979 Bryan Allen became the first man to cross the Channel in a man-powered aircraft, which he pedalled for 2 hours 49 minutes.

•

1994 Nicole Brown Simpson, the estranged wife of OJ Simpson, was found murdered in Los Angeles.

•

1997 the Globe Theatre in London reopened.

13 JUNE

1842 on a journey from Slough to Paddington, Queen Victoria became the first British monarch to travel by train.

•

1864 the Hammersmith and City railway opened in London.

•

1930 Sir Henry Segrave, holder of speed records on land and water, was killed on Windermere, Cumbria.

•

1944 the first flying bomb, the V1, hit London, killing six people in Hackney.

•

1951 Princess Elizabeth laid the foundation stone of the National Theatre on the South Bank, London.

•

1983 the US spacecraft *Pioneer 10* crossed the orbit of Neptune to become the first man-made object to leave the solar system.

14 JUNE

1381 during the Peasants' Revolt, protesters presented King Richard II with a series of demands.

•

1645 the Royalists were defeated by Cromwell's New Model Army at the Battle of Naseby in Northamptonshire.

•

1775 America's Second Continental Congress authorised the enlistment of ten companies of citizen-soldiers, an event regarded as the foundation of the US army.

•

1919 Captain John Alcock and Lieutenant Arthur Whitten Brown took off from Newfoundland on the first non-stop transatlantic flight.

•

1940 German troops marched into Paris.

•

1958 Nelson Mandela married Winnie Madikizela.

•

1982 the surrender of the Argentine forces ended the Falklands conflict.

15 JUNE

1215 King John set his seal on Magna Carta at Runnymede.

•

1825 the Duke of York laid the foundation stone of the new London Bridge.

•

1844 Charles Goodyear patented vulcanised rubber.

•

1896 a 110ft-high tsunami struck the coastline at Sanriku, Japan, claiming 27,000 lives.

•

1904 more than 1,000 people died when a fire broke out aboard the steamship *General Slocum* in the East River.

•

1996 in Manchester, the IRA exploded a 1,500kg bomb, the biggest detonated in Britain since the Second World War, causing £700 million of damage and injuring 200 people.

16 JUNE

1846 Pope Pius IX was elected, beginning the longest reign in the history of the papacy (31 years).

•

1884 the first purpose-built roller coaster, the Switchback Railway, opened in Coney Island, New York.

•

1903 the Ford Motor Company was founded.

•

1903 the trade name Pepsi-Cola was registered.

•

1917 the first All-Russia Congress of Soviets was convened.

•

1963 the Soviet Union launched the first woman into space: 26-year-old Valentina Tereshkova.

•

1992 the journalist Andrew Morton published *Diana: Her True Story* which claimed that the Princess of Wales had attempted suicide.

17 JUNE

1579 Sir Francis Drake, on his way to becoming the first Englishman to circumnavigate the globe, claimed Nova Albion (California) on behalf of Queen Elizabeth I.

•

1631 Mumtaz Mahal, wife of Shah Jahan, died in childbirth.

•

1940 German aircraft sank the Cunard liner the *Lancastria* off Saint-Nazaire, with the loss of more than 3,000 troops and refugees.

•

1950 the first kidney transplant took place in Chicago.

•

1970 Edwin Land patented the Polaroid camera.

•

1994 after a televised car chase, OJ Simpson was arrested for the murders of his former wife Nicole and her friend Ronald Goodman.

18 JUNE

1583 the first life insurance policy, on the life of William Gybbons, was issued in London.

•

1815 the French were defeated at the Battle of Waterloo.

•

1885 the Statue of Liberty, a gift from France to the US, arrived in New York.

•

1982 the body of Italian banker Roberto Calvi was found hanging beneath Blackfriars Bridge, London.

•

1984 5,000 striking miners clashed violently with police at Orgreave Colliery, Rotherham.

•

1996 as the US Senate's Whitewater committee issued its final report, Republicans and Democrats remained divided over whether the Clintons had committed any ethical breaches.

19 JUNE

1829 the Metropolitan Police Act received the royal assent, creating a new metropolitan police force that became known as Peelers or Bobbies.

•

1910 the first Zeppelin, *Deutschland*, was launched.

•

1953 Julius and Ethel Rosenberg were executed at Sing Sing Prison, New York, for spying for the Soviet Union.

•

1975 an inquest jury ruled that the missing Lord Lucan had murdered his children's nanny, Sandra Rivett.

•

1997 William Hague became the youngest leader of the Conservative Party in just over 200 years.

•

2012 Julian Assange, founder of WikiLeaks, sought asylum from the US in Ecuador's embassy in London.

1248 Oxford University gained its royal charter.

•

1756 British prisoners of the Nawab of Bengal suffocated in the Black Hole of Calcutta.

•

1791 King Louis XVI was captured attempting to flee from revolutionary Paris.

•

1837 Queen Victoria acceded to the throne, following the death of her uncle, King William IV.

•

1900 during the Boxer Rebellion, Chinese troops began a siege of the European Legation Quarter in Peking.

•

1975 *Jaws* was released in cinemas.

•

1984 it was announced that O-Levels would be replaced by the GCSE exam.

•

1990 a ticker-tape parade in New York honoured Nelson Mandela.

21 JUNE

1675 the foundation stone of the new St Paul's Cathedral was laid.

·

1919 the German fleet was scuttled at Scapa Flow, Orkney.

·

1937 lawn tennis at Wimbledon was televised for the first time.

·

1942 Tobruk fell to Rommel with the capture of 30,000 Allied troops.

·

1963 Cardinal Giovanni Battista Montini was elected Pope and took the name Paul VI.

·

1978 the musical *Evita* opened in London.

·

1982 Prince William was born.

·

2005 Klu Klux Klan member Edgar Ray Killen was convicted of having murdered three civil rights workers in Mississippi on this day in 1964.

22 JUNE

1633 the Inquisition forced Galileo Galilei to deny
his belief that the sun was the centre of the Universe.

•

1808 a duel in which the protagonists fired blunderbusses
at each other's hot-air balloons took place in Paris, with
tragic consequences for one combatant.

•

1814 Marylebone Cricket Club and Hertfordshire
played the first match at Lord's cricket ground in
St John's Wood, London.

•

1940 France and Germany signed an armistice.

•

1941 Hitler invaded the Soviet Union.

•

1979 the former Liberal Party leader Jeremy Thorpe
was cleared of the attempted murder of Norman Scott.

•

1990 Checkpoint Charlie closed.

23 JUNE

1626 a religious treatise found in the stomach of a fish was delivered to the University of Cambridge and eventually printed under the title *Vox Piscis*.

•

1757 British troops under Robert Clive defeated the Nawab of Bengal at the Battle of Plassey.

•

1956 Gamal Abdel Nasser was elected president of Egypt.

•

1972 Edward Heath's chancellor of the exchequer, Anthony Barber, announced that he would float the pound.

•

1985 an Air India jet disintegrated in mid-air off Ireland, killing all 329 people on board.

•

1992 John Gotti was sentenced to life in prison after being convicted of racketeering charges.

24 JUNE

1314 Robert Bruce's forces defeated the English under King Edward II at Bannockburn.

•

1717 the Grand Lodge of English Freemasons was formed.

•

1916 Mary Pickford became the first female film star to sign a contract for a million dollars.

•

1948 Soviet forces imposed a blockade between Allied-controlled Berlin and the West.

•

1971 the Mersey Tunnel was opened by the Queen, who named it Kingsway in honour of her father, King George VI.

•

2010 at Wimbledon, John Isner beat Nicholas Mahut 70–68 in the final set of the longest professional tennis match in history.

25 JUNE

1857 Baudelaire's *Les Fleurs du Mal* was published.

•

1876 General George Custer made his Last Stand as the 7th Cavalry were defeated by Sioux and Cheyenne warriors at Little Bighorn River, Montana, US.

•

1917 14,000 American troops landed in France.

•

1925 a prototype car telephone was exhibited in Germany.

•

1950 North Korean forces invaded South Korea.

•

1973 President Nixon and Leonid Brezhnev issued a communiqué at the close of the Soviet leader's US visit.

•

1997 Jacques-Yves Cousteau, underwater explorer, inventor of the aqualung and, in the words of President Chirac, the world's most famous Frenchman, died.

26 JUNE

1483 Richard III became king of England.

•

1857 the first Victoria Crosses were awarded,
in Hyde Park, London.

•

1906 the first motor racing grand prix took place
at Le Mans, France.

•

1913 Emily Dawson was appointed London's first
female magistrate.

•

1959 the Queen and US president Eisenhower opened
the St Lawrence Seaway, linking the Atlantic Ocean with
the Great Lakes of North America.

•

1960 Somaliland gained its independence from Britain.

•

1963 President John F Kennedy made his Ich bin ein
Berliner speech.

•

1977 in Indianapolis, Indiana, Elvis Presley gave his final
concert performance, two months before his death.

27 JUNE

1787 the historian Edward Gibbon completed his magnum opus, *The History of the Decline and Fall of the Roman Empire*.

•

1905 during the war with Japan, a mutiny erupted on board the Russian battleship *Potemkin* in the Black Sea.

•

1954 the world's first atomic power station began producing electricity in Obninsk, Soviet Union.

•

1957 the Medical Research Council concluded that there was a causal link between smoking and lung cancer.

•

1976 terrorists hijacked a French Airbus forcing it to land in Entebbe, Uganda.

•

2007 after ten years in office, Tony Blair resigned as prime minister.

28 JUNE

1461 Edward IV was crowned king.

·

1838 Queen Victoria was crowned in Westminster Abbey.

·

1859 the first dog show was held in England,
at Newcastle-upon-Tyne.

·

1914 Archduke Franz Ferdinand of Austria and his wife
Sophie were assassinated in Sarajevo.

·

1919 the Peace Treaty between the Allies and Germany
was signed in the Palace of Versailles.

·

1935 US president Roosevelt ordered a federal gold vault
to be built at Fort Knox, Kentucky.

·

1997 in a boxing bout against Evander Holyfield, the former
champion Mike Tyson was disqualified for biting a piece
from his opponent's ear.

29 JUNE

1871 the Trade Union Act legalised trade unions.

•

1905 motoring enthusiasts formed the
Automobile Association.

•

1916 the Irish nationalist Sir Roger Casement, arrested
after landing in Ireland from a German submarine,
was convicted of treason and sentenced to death.

•

1934 Hitler's Night of the Long Knives broke the power
of the SA (Stormtroopers).

•

1950 in Brazil, England lost 1–0 to USA, which some still
consider the greatest upset in World Cup history.

•

1986 Richard Branson's boat *Virgin Atlantic Challenger II*
crossed the Atlantic in a record 3 days 8 hours and
31 minutes.

1894 Tower Bridge in London was opened.

•

1936 Margaret Mitchell's *Gone With the Wind* was published.

•

1937 the number 999 was introduced for calls to the emergency services.

•

1960 the Republic of the Congo, formerly the Belgian Congo, gained its independence.

•

1971 three Russian cosmonauts were found dead in their space capsule when it landed in Kazakhstan, their cabin having become depressurised.

•

1985 after almost three weeks as captives of an Islamic militia following the hijacking of a TWA flight, 39 US hostages were released in Beirut.

•

1997 Hong Kong reverted to Chinese rule.

1 JULY

1690 the forces of King William III defeated those
of King James II at the Battle of the Boyne, Ireland.

·

1837 the registration of births, marriages and deaths
began in England and Wales.

·

1867 the British North America Act that created
the dominion of Canada came into effect.

·

1916 the first Battle of the Somme began and by the end
of the heaviest day of casualties in British military history
20,000 British soldiers were dead and 40,000 wounded.

·

1967 BBC2 began colour television broadcasts.

·

1969 Prince Charles was invested as Prince of Wales
at Caernarfon Castle.

1644 the Battle of Marston Moor turned the tide of the English Civil War in Oliver Cromwell's favour.

•

1819 the Factory Act was passed, prohibiting the employment of children under 9 in British textile factories and of children under 16 for more than 12 hours a day.

•

1900 Jean Sibelius's *Finlandia* was performed for the first time, in Helsinki.

•

1964 US president Lyndon Johnson signed the Civil Rights Act, banning racial discrimination.

•

2002 the adventurer Steve Fossett completed the first non-stop circumnavigation of the globe in a hot-air balloon.

•

2005 the Live8 charity concerts were held.

3 JULY

1608 the French navigator Samuel de Champlain founded and named Quebec.

•

1928 in London, John Logie Baird demonstrated the first colour television transmission.

•

1938 setting a speed record for steam locomotives, the London and North Eastern Railway's Mallard reached 126mph.

•

1971 the singer Jim Morrison, of The Doors, died of heart failure in Paris, aged 27.

•

1988 a US warship in The Gulf mistakenly shot down an Iranian passenger jet.

•

1996 John Major announced that the Stone of Scone, an ancient symbol of Scottish kings, would be removed from Westminster Abbey and return to Scotland after 700 years.

4 JULY

1054 Chinese astronomers recorded a supernova, visible for almost two years.

•

1776 the Continental Congress approved the US Declaration of Independence.

•

1826 former US presidents Thomas Jefferson and John Adams both died.

•

1944 the Russian army captured Minsk, the last major Soviet city in German hands.

•

1954 food rationing came to an end in Britain.

•

1976 Israeli commandos freed 103 hostages held by terrorists at Entebbe airport in Uganda.

•

1987 former Gestapo officer Klaus Barbie was sentenced to life imprisonment by a French court.

5 JULY

1841 the first guided tour was organised by Thomas Cook, when a train took about 500 temperance supporters 12 miles and back for one shilling.

•

1948 the NHS was created.

•

1954 the BBC broadcast its first daily TV news bulletin.

•

1969 the Rolling Stones gave a free concert in Hyde Park in London, attended by more than 350,000 people, in memory of Brian Jones, who had died two days before.

•

1975 Arthur Ashe became the first black tennis player to win the Wimbledon men's singles title, defeating Jimmy Connors.

•

1981 large-scale riots broke out in Toxteth, Liverpool.

6 JULY

1685 the Duke of Monmouth's rebellious forces were routed at the Battle of Sedgemoor by those of King James II.

•

1699 Captain William Kidd, pirate, was captured in America and deported to England, where he was executed.

•

1885 Louis Pasteur successfully tested his anti-rabies vaccine.

•

1952 trams disappeared from London's streets after being in use for almost a century.

•

1964 Nyasaland gained independence and a new name, Malawi.

•

1988 explosions on the North Sea oil rig Piper Alpha killed 167 men.

•

2005 it was announced that London would host the 2012 Olympic Games.

7 JULY

1865 Mary Surratt was hanged for conspiring to kill President Lincoln.

•

1967 Francis Chichester, who in May had completed his epic single-handed voyage around the world, was knighted by the Queen using Sir Francis Drake's sword.

•

1981 the first solar-powered aircraft, *Solar Challenger,* crossed the Channel.

•

1985 Boris Becker won his first Wimbledon title at 17, the youngest player to do so.

•

2005 suicide bombers set off four devices on the Tube and a London bus, killing 52 people and injuring 700.

•

2006 approaching 50, Martina Navratilova played her last match at Wimbledon.

8 JULY

1497 the Portuguese navigator Vasco da Gama set sail from Lisbon in search of a sea route to India.

•

1884 the first Society for the Prevention of Cruelty to Children was founded, later becoming the NSPCC.

•

1892 fingerprints were found at a murder scene in Buenos Aires, leading to the first conviction on fingerprint evidence.

•

1918 National Savings stamps went on sale.

•

1923 Virginia Woolf finished typesetting the first English edition of TS Eliot's *The Waste Land* for the Hogarth Press.

•

1990 Martina Navratilova defeated Zina Garrison and won her record ninth Wimbledon women's singles title.

9 JULY

1540 the marriage of King Henry VIII and Anne of Cleves was annulled after six months.

•

1917 the British battleship HMS *Vanguard* blew up in Scapa Flow, with the loss of more than 800 men.

•

1943 Allied troops began airborne landings in Sicily.

•

1951 Dashiell Hammett, author of *The Maltese Falcon*, was sentenced to six months in prison for contempt of court, having refused to give testimony that would help to trace communists accused of conspiring against the US.

•

1982 Michael Fagan, an unemployed father of four, broke into Buckingham Palace and made his way to the Queen's bedroom.

138 the Emperor Hadrian died at Baiae, in the Gulf of Naples, aged 62.

•

1940 in France, the Vichy government was instituted.

1947 the engagement was announced between Princess Elizabeth and Lieutenant Philip Mountbatten.

•

1962 the world's first communications satellite, Telstar, was launched from Cape Canaveral, Florida.

•

1970 David Broome, riding Beethoven, became the first Briton to win the world showjumping championship.

•

1973 the Bahamas gained their independence from Britain.

•

1985 a Greenpeace crew member died when the ship *Rainbow Warrior* was blown up by French secret agents in New Zealand.

11 JULY

1818 John Keats visited Robert Burns's birthplace
in Alloway, Ayrshire, and composed his sonnet,
Written in the Cottage Where Burns Was Born.

•

1897 the scientist Saloman Andrée left Spitsbergen by
balloon in a doomed attempt at Arctic exploration by air.

•

1960 the novel *To Kill a Mockingbird*, by Harper Lee,
was published.

•

1975 Chinese archaeologists announced the uncovering
of the terracotta army near the ancient capital of Xian.

•

1995 in Srebrenica, Bosnian Serb forces overran Dutch
peacekeepers and killed 8,000 Muslim men and boys in the
largest genocide in Europe since the Second World War.

12 JULY

100 BC Julius Caesar was born in Rome.

•

1543 King Henry VIII married Catherine Parr, his sixth and last wife.

•

1776 Captain James Cook set sail on his last voyage to try to locate the Northwest Passage.

•

1843 according to Joseph Smith, the leader of the Mormon Church, God conveyed to him the permissibility of polygamy.

•

1974 Bill Shankly retired as manager of Liverpool FC.

•

1990 the Russian president Boris Yeltsin resigned from the Soviet Communist Party.

•

1996 the Prince and Princess of Wales announced their intention to start divorce proceedings.

13 JULY

1878 at the conclusion of the Russo-Turkish War,
the Treaty of Berlin was signed, which failed to bring
lasting peace to the Balkans.

•

1930 Fifa's first World Cup tournament began in
Montevideo, Uruguay (and on July 30 was won by the
host nation).

•

1955 the convicted murderer Ruth Ellis was hanged
at Holloway prison in London, becoming the last woman
to be executed in the UK.

•

1985 Live Aid concerts took place simultaneously in
London and Philadelphia to raise money for famine relief
in Africa.

•

2016 David Cameron resigned as prime minister.

14 JULY

1789 the Bastille, Paris, was stormed and destroyed by the citizens.

•

1865 the British climber Edward Whymper led the first team to reach the summit of the Matterhorn.

•

1867 Alfred Nobel demonstrated dynamite for the first time at a quarry in Redhill, Surrey.

•

1902 the campanile of St Mark's Cathedral, Venice, collapsed during a safety inspection.

•

1930 BBC Television transmitted, from the Baird studios in Long Acre, London, its first play, *The Man with a Flower in His Mouth*, by Luigi Pirandello.

•

1965 Yvette Vaucher became the first woman to reach the Matterhorn's summit.

15 JULY

971 St Swithin's remains were moved, in torrential rain, from a church in Winchester to the newly built cathedral.

•

1099 the First Crusade succeeded in taking Jerusalem after a five-week siege, and massacred the city's Muslims and Jews.

•

1662 the Royal Society received its charter.

•

1815 Napoleon Bonaparte surrendered to Frederick Lewis Maitland, the captain of HMS *Bellerophon*.

•

1966 managers at Euston station, London, overturned a ban on black workers.

•

1997 the fashion designer Gianni Versace was murdered on the steps of his house in Miami, aged 50.

16 JULY

1661 the first banknotes in Europe were issued by the Bank of Stockholm.

·

1867 the Parisian Joseph Monier patented reinforced concrete.

·

1945 the first atomic bomb was detonated at Los Alamos, New Mexico.

·

1964 the Rolling Stones had their first UK No 1 hit with *It's All Over Now*.

·

1965 the Mont Blanc road tunnel opened, connecting France and Italy.

·

1994 the comet Shoemaker-Levy 9 collided with the planet Jupiter — the first collision of two solar system bodies to be observed.

·

1999 John F Kennedy Jr, son of President Kennedy, died when his light aircraft crashed.

17 JULY

709 BC the world's first record of a solar eclipse was made in China.

•

1917 the royal family changed its name from the House of Saxe-Coburg-Gotha to the House of Windsor.

•

1918 Tsar Nicholas II of Russia and his family were murdered by Bolsheviks.

•

1936 the Spanish generals Francisco Franco and Emilio Mola led the right-wing uprising that brought civil war.

•

1959 anthropologist Mary Leakey found the skull of a hominid now known as Australopithecus boisei in Tanzania.

•

1974 an explosion in the Tower of London killed one person and injured 41 people.

18 JULY

64 the great fire of Rome began, while Nero reputedly played the fiddle.

•

1863 the first Union regiment of black soldiers, the 54th Massachusetts Infantry, incurred 281 casualties while attacking Confederate positions.

•

1870 Pope Pius IX promulgated the dogma of papal infallibility.

•

1925 Adolf Hitler published *A Reckoning*, the first volume of *Mein Kampf*.

•

1955 Disneyland opened in California.

•

1969 US Senator Edward Kennedy's car crashed off a bridge in Massachusetts, killing Mary Jo Kopechne.

•

1976 Nadia Comaneci became the first person in Olympic Games history to score a perfect ten in gymnastics.

19 JULY

1545 the *Mary Rose*, pride of Henry VIII's fleet, sank in the Solent with the loss of more than 350 lives.

•

1588 the Spanish Armada was sighted off the Cornish coast.

•

1843 loose trousers for women were introduced by an American, Amelia Jenks Bloomer.

•

1843 the first all-metal liner, Isambard Kingdom Brunel's SS *Great Britain*, was launched in Bristol.

•

1919 a temporary wood and plaster Cenotaph was unveiled in Whitehall, London, in time for the march past that day by troops commemorating the end of the First World War.

1837 Euston station in London was opened by London and Birmingham Railway.

•

1944 Claus Schenk Graf von Stauffenberg attempted to assassinate Hitler with a bomb concealed in a briefcase.

•

1973 the film star and martial artist Bruce Lee died aged 32.

•

1974 Turkish forces invaded Cyprus.

•

1976 Nasa's *Viking 1* robot spacecraft landed on Mars.

•

1982 two IRA bombs placed in Hyde Park and Regent's Park killed eight soldiers on ceremonial duty, and seven horses.

•

1992 Vaclav Havel stepped down as president of Czechoslovakia as the country moved towards division into the Czech Republic and Slovakia.

21 JULY

1897 the Tate Gallery opened in London.

•

1904 the Trans-Siberian Railway was completed after 13 years' work.

•

1960 Francis Chichester arrived in New York aboard *Gipsy Moth III*, having set a record of 40 days for a solo Atlantic crossing.

•

1960 in Ceylon (now Sri Lanka) Sirima Bandaranaike became the world's first female prime minister, succeeding her assassinated husband Solomon.

•

1969 Neil Armstrong became the first person to walk on the moon.

•

1970 work was completed on the Aswan Dam after 11 years.

•

2005 public transport in London was targeted by four bombs which failed to explode properly.

1298 King Edward I's English troops defeated the Scots led by William Wallace at the Battle of Falkirk.

•

1933 the American pilot Wiley Post completed the first solo round-the-world flight in 7 days, 18 hours and 49 minutes.

•

1942 rationing of petrol began in the US after voluntary efforts failed.

•

1943 US forces under General George S Patton captured Palermo, Sicily.

•

1977 after the death of Chairman Mao and the fall of the Gang of Four, the previously disgraced Deng Xiaoping returned to power.

•

1990 England's Nick Faldo won The Open golf championship.

23 JULY

1952 a military coup took place in Egypt, led by General Muhammad Naguib, who deposed King Farouk I.

.

1974 Greece's military junta collapsed and former prime minister Constantine Karamanlis was asked to return from exile in Paris.

.

1986 Prince Andrew married Sarah Ferguson at Westminster Abbey.

.

1994 after 20 years of exile, the writer Alexander Solzhenitsyn arrived in Moscow.

.

1995 the Hale-Bopp comet was discovered.

.

1998 a team of scientists, led by Ryuzo Yanagimachi of the University of Hawaii, announced in the science journal *Nature* that they had produced three generations of cloned mice.

24 JULY

1534 Jacques Cartier landed in Canada, claiming the territory for France.

•

1567 Mary Queen of Scots abdicated and was succeeded by her infant son, James VI.

•

1704 during the War of the Spanish Succession, Gibraltar was captured by English and Dutch forces.

•

1847 the Mormons, driven from Illinois, reached the Salt Lake valley.

•

1958 the first life peerages were announced.

•

1967 Graham Greene, Francis Crick and the Beatles were among those who signed a full-page advertisement in *The Times* proclaiming the law against marijuana to be immoral in principle and unworkable in practice.

25 JULY

1797 Nelson's right arm was shattered by grapeshot in an assault on Tenerife and later had to be amputated.

•

1943 Benito Mussolini was forced to quit as prime minister of Italy.

•

1978 the world's first test-tube baby, Louise Joy Brown, was born in Oldham General Hospital, Greater Manchester.

•

1984 the Soviet cosmonaut Svetlana Savitskaya became the first woman to walk in space.

•

1992 the Olympic Games opened in Barcelona with all countries present for the first time in modern history.

•

2000 an Air France Concorde crashed soon after take-off in Paris, killing 113.

26 JULY

1908 the Federal Bureau of Investigation (FBI) was formed in Washington DC.

•

1945 Labour Party leader Clement Attlee was elected prime minister, toppling Winston Churchill.

•

1948 Britain's Freddie Mills became the world light heavyweight boxing champion when he beat the American Gus Lesnevich.

•

1952 Eva Perón died of cancer in Argentina at the age of 33.

•

1956 President Nasser of Egypt nationalised the Suez Canal, provoking a confrontation with Britain, France and Israel.

•

1983 Victoria Gillick lost her High Court attempt to prevent doctors prescribing contraception to under-16s without parental consent.

27 JULY

1694 the Bank of England's royal charter was sealed.

·

1890 the artist Vincent Van Gogh shot himself, dying two days later.

·

1921 University of Toronto researchers led by the biochemist Frederick Banting announced the discovery of the hormone insulin.

·

1953 the Korean armistice was signed in Panmunjom, ending three years of war.

·

1965 Edward Heath became the new Tory leader after the resignation of Sir Alec Douglas-Home.

·

1996 one person died when a bomb exploded during the Olympic Games, held in Atlanta, Georgia.

·

2000 the Labour government published its ten-year plan for revolutionising the NHS.

28 JULY

1588 the English fleet used fire ships to scatter the Spanish Armada.

•

1794 Maximilien Robespierre was guillotined.

•

1851 a total solar eclipse was captured on a daguerreotype photograph.

•

1858 fingerprints were used for the first time to identify a party to a contract.

•

1868 the 14th Amendment to the US Constitution was ratified, granting citizenship to former slaves.

•

1883 a water tricycle with paddlewheels was pedalled across the English Channel in less than eight hours, from Dover to Calais.

•

1914 Austria-Hungary declared war on Serbia.

•

1951 Walt Disney's cartoon *Alice In Wonderland* was released.

1565 Mary Queen of Scots married her cousin,
Lord Darnley.

•

1588 Sir Francis Drake, having been told of the sighting
of the Spanish Armada, put to sea with the English fleet.

•

1948 the first Olympic Games since the Second World War
opened at Wembley.

•

1949 BBC Television broadcast its first weather forecast.

•

1956 *Calypso*, the vessel of the underwater explorer
Jacques Cousteau, anchored in a record 7,500m of water.

•

1965 the Queen attended the premiere of the Beatles'
film *Help!*

•

1981 the Prince of Wales married Lady Diana Spencer.

30 JULY

1619 the first representative assembly in the Americas, the House of Burgesses, convened in Jamestown, Virginia.

•

1935 the first Penguin paperback, a biography of Shelley, was published.

•

1945 the Japanese submarine *I-58* sank the USS *Indianapolis*, killing 883 seamen.

•

1966 England won the football World Cup.

•

1974 President Richard Nixon released subpoenaed White House recordings after being ordered to do so by the Supreme Court.

•

1991 Pavarotti sang in the rain in a free concert in Hyde Park, London.

•

2006 *Top of the Pops* was broadcast for the last time after 42 years.

1498 Columbus, on his third voyage of exploration, arrived at an island which he named Trinidad.

•

1910 Dr Hawley Crippen and his mistress, Ethel Le Neve, disguised as a boy, were arrested on board the SS *Montrose*, for the murder of his wife.

•

1917 the third Battle of Ypres (Passchendaele) began.

•

1965 the last cigarette commercial appeared on British television.

•

1970 the daily rum ration was distributed for the last time in the Royal Navy.

•

2007 after 38 years, the longest continuous operation in its history, the British Army left Northern Ireland.

1 AUGUST

1774 Joseph Priestley, a Presbyterian minister and chemist, identified a gas that was later named oxygen.

•

1798 Nelson defeated the French at the Battle of the Nile.

•

1831 a new London Bridge, since replaced, opened to traffic.

•

1834 the British Empire began gradually to abolish slavery.

•

1907 the first camp for Scouts was held, on Brownsea Island, Poole.

•

1936 Hitler presided over the opening of the Berlin Olympic Games.

•

1944 the Warsaw Rising began against Nazi occupation.

•

2003 the Hutton inquiry opened into the death of weapons expert Dr David Kelly.

2 AUGUST

216 BC Hannibal defeated a much larger Roman army at Cannae, Italy.

•

1610 Henry Hudson discovered Hudson Bay while looking for the Northwest Passage.

•

1875 Britain's first roller-skating rink opened in Belgravia, London.

•

1939 Albert Einstein wrote to President Roosevelt regarding the urgency of conducting research into a nuclear bomb.

•

1943 *PT-109*, with future US president John F Kennedy aboard, was sunk in the Pacific.

•

1973 51 people died in a fire at the Summerland leisure resort, Douglas, Isle of Man.

•

1980 a bomb exploded at Bologna railway station, killing 85 people.

•

1990 Iraqi forces, 100,000-strong, invaded Kuwait.

3 AUGUST

1460 King James II of Scotland, who reigned 1437–60, was killed by an exploding cannon at the siege of Roxburgh Castle.

•

1904 British troops entered Lhasa, Tibet, forcing the Dalai Lama to take flight.

•

1914 Germany declared war on France.

•

1936 the American athlete Jesse Owens won the first of his four gold medals at the Berlin Olympics.

•

1958 the US atomic submarine *Nautilus* became the first vessel to reach the North Pole under the ice.

•

1990 a weather station at Nailstone, Leicestershire, recorded the highest temperature ever seen in Britain, 37.1C.

4 AUGUST

1693 champagne was invented by the Benedictine monk Dom Pierre Pérignon.

·

1870 at a public meeting in London, a resolution was passed calling for the formation of the British National Society for Aid to the Sick and Wounded in War (forerunner of the British Red Cross Society).

·

1914 Britain declared war on Germany.

·

1944 the diarist Anne Frank was arrested by the Gestapo.

·

1954 the prototype of Britain's first supersonic fighter aircraft, the English Electric Lightning, took to the air.

·

1964 two US destroyers report being attacked by North Vietnamese forces in the Gulf of Tonkin.

5 AUGUST

1891 the first traveller's cheque, devised by American Express, was cashed.

•

1926 the illusionist Harry Houdini spent 91 minutes underwater in a closed tank before escaping.

•

1962 Marilyn Monroe was found dead in bed.

•

1963 the Nuclear Test Ban Treaty was signed by Britain, America and Russia.

•

1973 a terrorist attack at Athens airport left three people dead and 55 wounded.

•

1975 the Forestry Commission reported the spread of dutch elm disease, which had infected three million trees.

•

1983 22 IRA members were jailed for a total of more than 4,000 years.

6 AUGUST

1806 the Holy Roman Empire was formally dissolved.

·

1890 the electric chair was used for the first time,
to execute the murderer William Kemmler in New York.

·

1945 the Americans dropped an atomic bomb
on Hiroshima.

·

1961 Russian cosmonaut Gherman Titov spent the day
in space, four months after Yuri Gagarin's historic trip.

·

1971 British sailor Chay Blyth became the first person
to sail single-handedly non-stop east to west around
the world.

·

1987 David Owen announced his resignation as leader
of the SDP.

·

1996 Nasa announced evidence of a primitive form
of microscopic life on Mars.

1840 an Act of Parliament prohibited the employment of boys as chimney sweeps.

•

1926 the first British motor racing grand prix was run at Brooklands.

•

1947 Thor Heyerdahl's *Kon-Tiki* raft landed in Polynesia after a journey of 4,300 miles across the Pacific.

•

1972 the Ugandan leader, Idi Amin, gave Ugandan Asians who were not citizens of the country 90 days in which to leave.

•

1987 Lynne Cox became the first person to swim from the US to the Soviet Union.

•

1998 230 people were killed in terrorist bombings at the US embassies in Nairobi and Dar es Salaam.

8 AUGUST

1834 the English Poor Law Act was passed, whereby relief would only be given in a workhouse.

•

1900 the first Davis Cup tennis competition, named after Dwight Filley Davis, began at the Longwood Cricket Club in Brookline, Massachusetts.

•

1963 £2.6 million was stolen from the Glasgow–London mail train at Cheddington, Buckinghamshire, in the Great Train Robbery.

•

1969 the Beatles posed for the photograph that became the cover of the *Abbey Road* LP.

•

1974 President Nixon announced his resignation after the Watergate affair.

•

1991 John McCarthy was released from captivity in Beirut after 1,943 days.

9 AUGUST

1173 construction began on what became the Leaning Tower of Pisa, the campanile of the city's cathedral.

•

1902 Edward VII was crowned king of the United Kingdom of Great Britain and Ireland.

•

1945 the Americans dropped an atomic bomb on Nagasaki, killing more than 35,000 people.

•

1969 the actress Sharon Tate and four of her friends were murdered in Los Angeles by the followers of Charles Manson.

•

1965 Singapore gained its independence from Malaysia.

•

1974 Gerald Ford became the 38th American president on Richard Nixon's resignation.

•

1999 Charles Kennedy succeeded Paddy Ashdown as leader of the Liberal Democrats.

10 AUGUST

1628 the Swedish warship *Vasa* sank off Stockholm on her maiden voyage.

·

1675 King Charles II laid the foundation stone of the Royal Observatory.

·

1793 the Louvre museum opened in Paris.

·

1846 the Smithsonian Institution was established in Washington DC, funded by a bequest from the British scientist James Smithson.

·

1904 the Japanese defeated the Russians off Port Arthur, in the Battle of the Yellow Sea.

·

1932 film star Rin Tin Tin, died aged 14 (98 in dog years).

·

1988 the US president, Ronald Reagan, signed the Civil Liberties Act, providing an apology to those of Japanese ancestry mistreated during the Second World War.

11 AUGUST

1942 film star Hedy Lamarr was granted a patent for frequency-hopping technology that later became the basis for wifi.

•

1952 Prince Hussein was proclaimed king of the Hashemite Kingdom of Jordan.

•

1982 gangsters the Kray twins were released from prison to attend their mothers' funeral.

•

1984 President Ronald Reagan, faced with a microphone which he wrongly believed not to be working, joked that the US was about to bomb the Soviet Union.

•

1984 the American favourite Mary Decker tangled with the barefoot Zola Budd and fell in the 3,000m at the Los Angeles Olympics.

12 AUGUST

3 a planetary conjunction was visible that may have been the Star of Bethlehem mentioned in the New Testament.

•

1851 Isaac Singer received a patent for his sewing machine.

•

1865 Joseph Lister became the first surgeon to use disinfectant during an operation.

•

1887 Thomas Edison made the first sound recording onto a foil-wrapped cylinder on the Edisonphone.

•

1960 Echo I, the first US communications satellite, was launched from Cape Canaveral.

•

1980 the first birth in captivity of a giant panda took place in a Mexican zoo.

•

1981 the IBM personal computer went on sale.

13 AUGUST

1704 the Duke of Marlborough, in command of an allied army, routed French and Bavarian forces at the Battle of Blenheim.

•

1876 Wagner's *Der Ring des Nibelungen* was first performed in its entirety in Bayreuth.

•

1913 stainless steel was first cast in Sheffield.

•

1961 the East Germans began building the Berlin Wall.

•

1964 Britain's last two executions of murderers took place, in Liverpool and Manchester.

•

1966 China announced plans for a "Great Leap Forward".

•

1977 more than 200 people were arrested in violent protests against the National Front in Lewisham, south London.

14 AUGUST

1040 King Duncan I of Scotland was killed in battle against his cousin Macbeth, near Elgin.

·

1811 Paraguay declared its independence from Spain.

·

1880 Cologne Cathedral was completed after 632 years.

·

1941 the Atlantic Charter was signed by Winston Churchill and Franklin Roosevelt.

·

1945 Japan unconditionally surrendered to the Allies.

·

1947 Pakistan became independent from Britain.

·

1975 the film *The Rocky Horror Picture Show*, which would become the longest-running in cinema history, was released.

·

2000 rescuers vainly tried to save the 118 crew of the Russian submarine *Kursk*, which had sunk in the Barents Sea.

15 AUGUST

1843 the Tivoli Pleasure Gardens opened in Copenhagen.

•

1914 the Panama Canal opened.

•

1945 VJ Day was celebrated, marking Japan's unconditional surrender to the Allies the previous day.

•

1947 India became independent from Britain.

•

1965 the Beatles played to 60,000 spectators at Shea Stadium, New York City.

•

1969 the Woodstock music festival began in Bethel, New York.

•

1971 showjumper Harvey Smith made a two-fingered gesture to judges after winning the British Show Jumping Derby, and was subsequently stripped of his title and winnings.

•

1998 a car bombing in Omagh, Northern Ireland, killed 29 people.

16 AUGUST

1819 the Peterloo massacre of protesters wanting parliamentary representation took place at St Peter's Field, Manchester.

•

1896 gold was discovered at Rabbit Creek in Yukon, Canada, sparking the gold rush.

•

1921 *The Times* exposed as a forgery the *Protocols of the Elders of Zion*, which had purported to be a manifesto outlining a Jewish conspiracy for world domination.

•

1960 Cyprus became an independent republic.

•

1962 drummer Pete Best left the Beatles and was subsequently replaced by Ringo Starr.

•

1977 Elvis Presley was found dead at his mansion in Memphis, Tennessee.

•

1984 carmaker John DeLorean was acquitted of drug trafficking charges.

17 AUGUST

1896 Mrs Bridget Driscoll of Croydon, Surrey, became the first pedestrian to be knocked down and killed by a motor vehicle in Britain.

•

1978 three Americans, Ben Abruzzo, Max Anderson and Larry Newman, landed in France, having made the first crossing of the Atlantic Ocean by hot-air balloon.

•

1987 Rudolf Hess, formerly Hitler's deputy, and the only inmate of Spandau prison, Berlin, committed suicide aged 93.

•

1998 President Clinton admitted having an inappropriate relationship with White House intern Monica Lewinsky.

•

1999 an earthquake registering 6.7 on the Richter scale struck Izmit in western Turkey, killing more than 17,000.

18 AUGUST

1612 the trial of the Pendle witches began at
Lancaster assizes.

•

1759 in the Battle of Lagos Bay, Portugal, a French fleet
was defeated by the British under Admiral Boscawen.

•

1932 Scottish aviator Jim Mollison made the first
westbound transatlantic solo flight.

•

1940 the peak of the Battle of Britain, later dubbed
the "Hardest Day", became the largest engagement
in the history of aerial warfare to date.

•

1941 Britain's National Fire Service was established.

•

1958 *Lolita* was published in the United States.

•

1960 the first oral contraceptive was launched in the
United States.

1960 a Soviet court sentenced Gary Powers, the American U2 spy plane pilot, to ten years' detention.

·

1960 the USSR launched the *Sputnik 5* spacecraft into orbit around Earth, carrying two dogs named Belka (Squirrel) and Strelka (Little Arrow).

·

1987 a gunman, Michael Ryan, killed 14 people in Hungerford, Berkshire.

·

1989 Solidarity's Tadeusz Mazowiecki was nominated as prime minister of Poland, making it the first country in eastern Europe to end one-party communist rule.

·

1991 Soviet Union hardliners attempted a coup against the president Mikhail Gorbachev.

·

2004 Google was listed as a public company.

20 AUGUST

1667 John Milton's *Paradise Lost* was entered in the Stationers' Register.

∙

1859 Charles Darwin published his theory of evolution by natural selection.

∙

1882 Tchaikovsky's *1812 Overture* received its premiere in Moscow.

∙

1940 Winston Churchill paid tribute to "the Few" in a speech.

∙

1968 Russian troops invaded Czechoslovakia.

∙

1970 England football captain Bobby Moore was acquitted of charges of stealing an emerald bracelet in Colombia shortly before the World Cup.

∙

1977 America's *Voyager II* spacecraft was launched to explore the outer planets.

∙

1989 51 people died when a dredger collided with the pleasure cruiser *Marchioness* on the River Thames.

1808 British and Portuguese forces led by Arthur Wellesley won the first battle of the Peninsular War, at Vimeiro.

•

1959 Hawaii became the 50th US state.

•

1961 country singer Patsy Cline recorded *Crazy*.

•

1963 martial law was declared in South Vietnam.

•

1983 the Philippines' opposition leader, Benigno Aquino Jr, was shot dead minutes after returning home from exile.

•

1986 more than 1,700 people were killed by a cloud of gas that escaped from the volcanic Lake Nyos in Cameroon, West Africa.

•

1988 British licensing laws were relaxed.

•

2013 hundreds of people died in chemical attacks in Ghouta, Syria.

1485 Henry Tudor defeated King Richard III at the Battle of Bosworth Field.

•

1642 when King Charles I raised his standard at Nottingham, the English Civil War is considered to have begun.

•

1770 Captain James Cook claimed eastern Australia as British territory.

•

1846 the United States annexed New Mexico.

•

1902 Henry Leland founded the Cadillac Motor Company in Detroit.

•

1960 Peter Cook, Dudley Moore, Alan Bennett and Jonathan Miller opened their satirical revue *Beyond the Fringe* at the Edinburgh Festival Fringe.

•

1985 55 people died in a fire on board a passenger plane at Manchester.

1617 the first one-way streets were established in London.

•

1873 the Albert Bridge over the Thames at Chelsea
was opened.

•

1921 the British airship *R-38* crashed in the Humber
estuary, killing all but four of her 49-man crew.

•

1939 Germany and the Soviet Union signed a
non-aggression pact.

•

1942 the Battle of Stalingrad began.

•

1979 the Bolshoi Ballet dancer Alexander Godunov sought
political asylum in New York.

•

1990 the Iraqi leader Saddam Hussein provoked outrage by
appearing with hostages on state television and ruffling the
hair of a young British boy.

79 Mount Vesuvius erupted, burying Pompeii and Herculaneum in volcanic ash.

•

410 Rome was overrun by the Visigoths.

•

1456 the Gutenberg Bible was printed.

•

1572 the slaughter of French Huguenots, known as the St Bartholomew's Day Massacre, began in Paris.

•

1690 Job Charnock, chief agent of the British East India Company, founded the city of Calcutta.

•

1814 British troops stormed Washington and set fire to the White House.

•

1875 Captain Matthew Webb from landlocked Shropshire became the first person to swim the English Channel.

•

1990 after four years, kidnappers released the Irish hostage Brian Keenan in Beirut.

25 AUGUST

1537 the oldest extant regiment in the British Army, the Honourable Artillery Company, was founded.

•

1940 the RAF bombed Berlin for the first time.

1944 General de Gaulle entered Paris following the German surrender.

1991 Linus Torvalds unveiled the first version of the Linux computer operating system.

•

1997 a Berlin court sentenced the former East German leader Egon Krenz to six and a half years in prison for instigating the shoot-to-kill policy of border guards at the Berlin Wall.

•

2012 *Voyager I* became the first man-made object to enter interstellar space.

26 AUGUST

55 BC Roman legionaries led by Julius Caesar landed in Britain.

•

1346 King Edward III, aided by his son the Black Prince, defeated the French at the Battle of Crécy.

•

1920 the US Secretary of State certified ratification of the 19th Amendment, giving American women the right to vote.

•

1936 the BBC transmited the first high-definition television pictures, from Alexandra Palace.

•

1974 Charles Lindbergh died aged 72.

•

1985 the South African-born athlete Zola Budd broke the 5,000m record by ten seconds at Crystal Palace.

•

1999 Russia began the second Chechen war following the invasion of Dagestan.

1576 the painter Titian died in Venice aged 88.

1783 Jacques Alexandre César Charles, a member of the French Academy of Science, launched the first balloon inflated with hydrogen gas.

1859 the first commercially productive oil well was drilled at Titusville, Pennsylvania.

1883 the Indonesian volcano Krakatoa erupted, killing more than 30,000 people.

1967 the Beatles' manager Brian Epstein died in Belgravia, London, aged 32.

1979 18 British soldiers were killed in an ambush at Warrenpoint, Northern Ireland, and an IRA bomb killed Lord Louis Mountbatten and three companions in his boat at Sligo.

28 AUGUST

1850 conducted by Franz Liszt, Wagner's opera *Lohengrin* received its premiere in Weimar.

•

1913 the Peace Palace in The Hague was officially opened.

•

1963 Martin Luther King Jr delivered his I Have a Dream speech to 200,000 people in Washington.

•

1972 the US swimmer Mark Spitz won the first of his seven gold medals at the Munich Olympics.

•

1972 Prince William of Gloucester was killed in an air crash.

•

1994 Sunday trading was legalised in England and Wales.

•

2004 Kelly Holmes won the double of the 800m and 1,500m titles at the Olympic Games in Athens.

1782 HMS *Royal George* keeled over at anchor in the Solent and sank with the loss of about 900 lives.

•

1831 Michael Faraday demonstrated the first electrical transformer.

•

1885 the first motorcycle was patented by Gottlieb Daimler in Germany.

•

1950 the first British soldiers arrived in Korea.

•

1965 astronauts Charles Conrad and Gordon Cooper splashed down in the Atlantic after nearly eight days orbiting Earth in *Gemini V*.

•

1966 the Beatles performed their last concert before paying fans in San Francisco.

•

2005 Hurricane Katrina struck the US Gulf Coast, killing nearly 2,000 people.

70 the siege of Jerusalem ended as the emperor Titus destroyed the Temple.

·

1901 Hubert Cecil Booth, a Scot, patented a vacuum cleaner which sucked in dust and retained it by means of a filter.

·

1914 the Russians were defeated by the Germans at Tannenberg.

·

1918 Vladimir Lenin survived an assassination attempt in Moscow, setting in motion the Red Terror.

·

1941 the siege of Leningrad began.

·

1963 the defector Guy Burgess died in Moscow, aged 52.

·

1976 more than 100 police officers were taken to hospital after clashes at the Notting Hill Carnival.

1888 the body of Mary Ann "Polly" Nichols, the first victim of Jack the Ripper, was found in London.

•

1900 Coca-Cola first went on sale in Britain.

•

1928 *The Threepenny Opera* by Kurt Weill and Bertolt Brecht was first performed in Berlin.

•

1936 Elizabeth Cowell became the first female television announcer, speaking on the BBC.

•

1994 the IRA announced it would cease military operations.

•

1997 Diana, Princess of Wales, and Dodi Fayed were killed in a car crash in Paris.

•

2005 almost 1,000 pilgrims were killed when a crowd panicked on a bridge in Baghdad.

1858 the East India Company's formal rule of India ended as the Crown took over its territories.

•

1879 Britain signed a peace agreement with the Zulu chiefs.

•

1920 France created the state of Lebanon.

•

1923 Japan was struck by an earthquake, resulting in 140,000 deaths.

•

1939 Germany invaded Poland, heralding the start of the Second World War.

•

1967 an Arab summit in Khartoum lifted the oil embargo on the West imposed during the Six Day War.

•

1983 a Korean airliner was shot down over Russia after straying off course, killing all on board.

2 SEPTEMBER

1666 the Great Fire of London began.

•

1752 Britain and its colonies replaced the Julian calendar with the Gregorian, so that September 3 became September 14.

•

1898 news was received of Sir Horatio Kitchener's reconquest of the Sudan.

•

1945 the Second World War ended when General Douglas MacArthur accepted the Japanese surrender on board the battleship, USS *Missouri*.

•

1954 the National Trust for Scotland acquired Fair Isle, an island known for its birdlife and knitted sweaters.

•

1963 George Wallace, governor of Alabama, halted integration of black and white students by surrounding Tuskegee High School with state troopers.

3 SEPTEMBER

301 San Marino, the oldest extant republic, was founded.

•

1651 at the Battle of Worcester, a Royalist army under King Charles II was defeated by Commonwealth forces under Cromwell.

•

1783 the Treaty of Versailles was signed by which Britain recognised the independence of the United States.

•

1909 the first Boy Scout rally was held at Crystal Palace, south London.

•

1939 Britain and France declared war on Germany.

•

1943 Allied troops invaded Italy.

•

1944 Anne Frank and her family were transported from the Netherlands to Auschwitz.

•

1976 the American *Viking II* spacecraft touched down on Mars.

4 SEPTEMBER

476 the Western Roman Empire ended after almost 500 years when Romulus Augustulus was deposed.

•

1733 Britain's first lioness died of old age in the Tower of London's Royal Menagerie.

•

1882 Thomas Edison turned on the first electrical plant, in Manhattan.

•

1888 George Eastman registered the trademark Kodak and took out a patent for the first roll-film camera.

•

1948 Wilhelmina, Queen of the Netherlands since 1890, abdicated in favour of her daughter, Juliana.

•

1964 the Queen opened the Forth Road Bridge.

•

1998 Google was founded by US students Larry Page and Sergey Brin.

5 SEPTEMBER

1666 the Great Fire of London was extinguished.

•

1774 America's first Continental Congress was convened in Philadelphia.

•

1800 French troops occupying Malta surrendered to the British.

•

1972 at the Olympic Games in Munich, Palestinian terrorists killed two members of the Israeli team and took nine more hostage, all of whom were killed in an ensuing battle.

•

1975 an apparent assassination attempt against the US president, Gerald R Ford, was foiled by a secret service agent.

•

1979 Lord Mountbatten was buried at Romsey, Hampshire, after a funeral at Westminster Abbey.

•

1997 Mother Teresa of Calcutta died aged 87.

6 SEPTEMBER

1879 the first public telephone exchange in Britain opened.

•

1901 William McKinley, the 25th American president (1897–1901), was shot in Buffalo, New York, leading to his death eight days later.

•

1948 test pilot John Douglas Derry became the first Briton to break the sound barrier.

•

1952 31 people were killed when a fighter jet, piloted by John Derry, broke up above spectators at the Farnborough air show.

•

1968 Swaziland (now Eswatini) gained its independence from Britain.

•

1997 after a public funeral in London, Diana, Princess of Wales, was buried in the grounds of Althorp, Northamptonshire.

7 SEPTEMBER

1191 King Richard I defeated Saladin at Arsuf.

•

1813 in a newspaper article in Troy, New York, the nickname Uncle Sam was first used to denote the United States.

•

1940 the Blitz began as the Luftwaffe bombed London for the first of 57 consecutive nights.

•

1953 Nikita Khrushchev became head of the Soviet Communist Party.

•

1978 Bulgarian dissident Georgi Markov was assassinated on Waterloo Bridge by a ricin pellet shot from an adapted umbrella.

•

1994 the lowering of the American flag over US army headquarters in Berlin formally ended American presence in the city after almost 50 years.

8 SEPTEMBER

1888 the first Football League matches took place.

•

1888 the body of Annie Chapman, the second victim of Jack the Ripper, was found.

•

1944 London was hit for the first time by a V2 rocket.

•

1966 the first episode of *Star Trek* was broadcast.

•

1974 US president Ford issued an unconditional pardon for any offences his predecessor Richard Nixon might have committed as president.

•

1986 General Augusto Pinochet, president of Chile, survived an attempt on his life.

•

1991 the electorate of the Yugoslav republic of Macedonia voted for their homeland to become an independent state.

9 SEPTEMBER

9 three Roman legions were destroyed by Arminius
in the Teutoburg forest, now in Germany.

•

1513 King James IV of Scotland was defeated and killed
by English troops at the Battle of Flodden Field.

•

1776 the United Colonies were renamed the United States
of America.

•

1850 California was admitted as the 31st state of the US.

•

1948 North Korea proclaimed its independence.

•

1956 Elvis Presley appeared for the first time on
The Ed Sullivan Show.

•

1976 China's leader Mao Zedong died aged 82.

•

2015 Queen Elizabeth II became the longest-reigning
British monarch.

10 SEPTEMBER

1897 London taxi-driver George Smith became the first person to be convicted for drink-driving.

•

1939 a week after Britain and France had declared war on Germany, Canada did the same.

•

1945 the Norwegian Vidkun Quisling was sentenced to death for collaborating with Nazi Germany.

•

1967 the people of Gibraltar voted in favour of remaining under British rule.

•

1981 Picasso's painting *Guernica* returned to Spain, having hung in New York since 1939.

•

2000 six hostages held in Sierra Leone were rescued by British forces.

•

2008 the Large Hadron Collider at CERN, Geneva, was switched on.

11 SEPTEMBER

1789 Alexander Hamilton became the first Secretary of the US Treasury.

•

1841 the first regular commuter train service between London and Brighton began.

•

1997 Scots voted in favour of a plan to give them their own assembly.

•

1998 Kenneth Starr's report on President Bill Clinton appeared on the internet, listing 11 potentially impeachable offences.

•

2001 four hijacked Boeing airliners were targeted against the World Trade Center in New York and the Pentagon in Washington DC, resulting in the loss of nearly 3,000 lives.

•

2003 Sweden's foreign minister Anna Lindh died after being stabbed in a Stockholm department store.

12 SEPTEMBER

1878 Cleopatra's Needle was erected on the Thames Embankment, London.

•

1942 a German U-boat sank the *Laconia*, a former British cruise ship carrying about 1,800 Italian prisoners-of-war.

1970 Concorde landed for the first time at Heathrow, giving rise to complaints about noise.

•

1974 Emperor Haile Selassie of Ethiopia was deposed by a military coup.

•

1990 East and West Germany and the Second World War Allies signed a treaty to restore sovereignty to a united Germany.

•

1992 the US space shuttle *Endeavour* took off with a crew that included the first married couple in space.

13 SEPTEMBER

1672 John Bunyan was released from Bedford prison after 12 years' imprisonment for non-conformist preaching.

•

1788 New York was declared the first federal capital of America.

•

1899 Henry Bliss, a real estate broker, was knocked down by a New York taxi cab, becoming the first recorded fatality from an automobile accident.

•

1922 the world's highest temperature in the shade, 58C (136F), was recorded at Al Aziziyah, Libya.

•

1982 Lindy Chamberlain, who claimed her missing baby had been taken by a dingo, went on trial.

•

2001 Iain Duncan Smith became leader of the Conservative Party.

14 SEPTEMBER

1321 Dante Alighieri died in Ravenna, Italy, aged 56.

•

1741 Handel finished his oratorio *Messiah* after 23 days' concentrated work.

•

1812 Napoleon entered Moscow.

•

1960 at a meeting in Baghdad, oil-producing countries founded OPEC.

•

1960 Mobutu Sese Soko seized power in the Congo.

•

1975 Elizabeth Ann Bayley Seton (1774–1821) became the first American citizen to be canonised.

•

1982 former Hollywood star Princess Grace of Monaco died of injuries sustained in a car accident.

•

2007 Northern Rock became the first British bank in 150 years to fail during a run as customers rushed to withdraw their savings.

1830 William Huskisson, MP for Liverpool, became the world's first railway fatality after an accident at the opening of the Liverpool & Manchester Railway.

•

1845 Henry Sweet, philologist, phonetician and the man upon whom Bernard Shaw based some aspects of Henry Higgins in *Pygmalion*, was born.

•

1916 the Battle of Flers-Courcelette, part of the Somme offensive, began, with the British using tanks for the first time.

•

1938 Neville Chamberlain visited Adolf Hitler at Berchtesgaden.

•

1940 RAF fighters claimed to have shot down 176 German aircraft in the decisive day of the Battle of Britain.

16 SEPTEMBER

1620 the Pilgrim Fathers set sail from Plymouth on the *Mayflower*.

•

1861 the Post Office Savings Bank was established.

1868 golf's first recorded hole-in-one was scored by Tom Morris at Prestwick during the Open Championships.

•

1974 the giant pandas Chia Chia and Ching Ching arrived at London Zoo from China.

•

1977 pop star Marc Bolan died in a car accident aged 29.

•

1992 Britain withdrew from the European Exchange Rate Mechanism on Black Wednesday.

•

1994 John Major lifted media restrictions on Sinn Fein.

•

2013 gunman Aaron Alexis killed 12 people at the Navy Yard in Washington DC.

17 SEPTEMBER

1394 Jews were expelled from France by order
of King Charles VI.

•

1683 the Dutch scientist Antony van Leeuwenhoek wrote
to the Royal Society reporting his discovery of live bacteria.

•

1944 Operation Market Garden began around Arnhem in
the Netherlands.

•

1953 the first successful separation of conjoined twins took
place at the Ochsner Foundation Hospital in New Orleans.

•

1976 Nasa unveiled *Enterprise*, the first space shuttle orbiter.

•

1978 Menachem Begin, the prime minister of Israel,
and Anwar Sadat, the president of Egypt, signed
a framework for a peace treaty, brokered by the US
president Jimmy Carter.

18 SEPTEMBER

1851 *The New York Times* was first published.

•

1891 Harriet Maxwell Converse became the first white woman to be the chief of an American Indian tribe.

•

1914 the third Irish Home Rule Bill received royal assent but its implementation was suspended.

•

1970 musician Jimi Hendrix died aged 27.

•

1975 the heiress Patti Hearst was arrested after taking part in criminal activities with the terrorist group that had kidnapped her six months previously.

•

1981 France abolished capital punishment and the guillotine.

•

1998 ICANN, the internet naming company, was formed. (ICANN – Internet Corporation for Assigned Names and Numbers.)

1876 American inventor Melville Bissell patented
the carpet sweeper.

•

1888 the world's first beauty contest was held in Belgium
and won by 18-year-old Bertha Soucaret from Guadeloupe.

•

1905 Thomas Barnardo, founder of the children's
charity, died.

•

1955 Juan Perón, president of Argentina since 1946,
resigned and went into exile in Paraguay.

•

1973 Paul Theroux left Victoria Station on the 3.30pm train
for Folkestone and Paris, beginning the journey chronicled
in his 1975 book *The Great Railway Bazaar*.

•

2000 the People's Fuel Lobby was formed at a meeting
in Altrincham, Cheshire, to protest against increased
petrol prices.

20 SEPTEMBER

1643 Robert Devereux, Earl of Essex, defeated the Royalist army at the first Battle of Newbury.

•

1853 Elisha Graves Otis opened a factory in New York State for the production of the first modern passenger lift.

•

1928 the Italian Chamber of Deputies was taken over by the Fascists.

•

1931 Britain came off the gold standard.

•

1946 the first Cannes film festival opened.

•

1973 Billie Jean King beat Bobby Riggs in the Battle of the Sexes tennis match.

•

1992 French voters narrowly approved the Maastricht Treaty.

•

2000 a missile was fired at MI6's headquarters in London.

1327 King Edward II died aged 43 at Berkeley Castle, Gloucestershire, reputedly murdered by his wife Isabella and her lover, Mortimer.

•

1745 Prince Charles Edward Stuart's troops defeated those of George II at Prestonpans in ten minutes.

•

1915 Stonehenge, and the surrounding 30 acres of land, were sold at auction for £6,600 to Mr Cecil Chubb, who later presented it to the nation.

•

1949 at Goodison Park, England suffered their first home defeat by a foreign football team with the Republic of Ireland winning 2–0.

•

1952 Sir Montague Burton, The Tailor of Taste, died aged 67.

22 SEPTEMBER

1735 Sir Robert Walpole became the first prime minister to reside at 10 Downing Street.

●

1862 the US president Abraham Lincoln declared that all slaves in rebellious states would be free from January 1, 1863.

●

1955 as Independent television began, the first TV commercial — for Gibbs SR toothpaste — was broadcast in Britain.

●

1985 France's prime minister, Laurent Fabius, admitted that French secret agents had sunk the Greenpeace ship *Rainbow Warrior* in New Zealand.

●

1996 Bob Dent, an Australian cancer victim, became the first man in the world to commit legally assisted suicide from a lethal injection.

23 SEPTEMBER

480 BC the Greeks defeated the Persian fleet at the Battle of Salamis.

•

1846 the astronomer Johan Galle discovered Neptune.

1889 Nintendo was founded as a playing-card company.

•

1909 *The Phantom of the Opera*, a story by Gaston Leroux, first began serialisation.

•

1940 the George Cross was instituted by King George VI for civilian acts of courage.

•

1974 Ceefax, the world's first teletext service, began on BBC television.

•

1987 an Australian court allowed Peter Wright to publish his banned memoir, *Spycatcher*.

•

2000 in Sydney, oarsman Steve Redgrave won gold at a fifth consecutive Olympic Games.

1776 the St Leger horse race was run for the first time in Doncaster.

•

1930 *Private Lives* by Noël Coward was first performed in London.

•

1940 a German bomb nearly stopped production of *The Times* for the first time since 1785.

•

1960 the first nuclear-powered aircraft carrier, the USS *Enterprise*, was launched at Newport, Virginia.

•

1971 90 Russian diplomats were expelled from Britain for spying.

•

1975 Doug Haston and Doug Scott became the first Britons to summit Mount Everest.

•

1992 David Mellor resigned as heritage minister in the wake of revelations about his way of life.

25 SEPTEMBER

1818 the first transfusion using human blood was performed by James Blundell at Guy's Hospital in London.

•

1849 composer of waltzes Johann Strauss I died aged 45.

•

1878 Dr Charles Drysdale, senior physician to the Metropolitan Free Hospital, wrote in *The Times* that the use of tobacco is one of the most evident of all the retrograde influences of our time.

•

1897 Britain's first motor bus service started in Bradford.

•

1932 Catalonia became autonomous with its own parliament, language and flag.

•

1997 the British Thrust SuperSonic car set a new land-speed record in Nevada of 714.1mph.

1580 Sir Francis Drake completed his circumnavigation of the globe.

•

1687 while Ottoman forces in Athens were under attack by Venetian troops, the Parthenon, which was used as a gunpowder magazine, was partly destroyed when a shell landed on it.

•

1907 New Zealand changed from a colony to an independent dominion.

•

1934 Queen Mary launched RMS *Queen Mary* at Clydebank, Scotland.

•

1957 the Bernstein-Sondheim musical *West Side Story* was first performed in New York.

•

1969 the Beatles released the final LP they recorded together, *Abbey Road*.

•

1977 Freddie Laker's Skytrain took off from Gatwick for New York with tickets for £59.

27 SEPTEMBER

1540 the Society of Jesus (the Jesuits) was founded.

•

1825 the Stockton-Darlington railway opened.

1888 a letter signed Jack the Ripper, assumed to be a hoax triggered by the murders in the East End, was received by the Central News Agency.

•

1922 Constantine I, King of Greece, abdicated after Greece lost the Greco-Turkish War of 1919–22.

•

1960 Europe's first moving pavement, the travelator, opened at Bank station.

•

1968 the musical *Hair* opened in London a day after theatre censorship ended in Britain.

•

1975 five members of militant groups were executed by firing squad in Spain, leading to an outcry.

1745 *God Save the King* was sung for the first time at the Drury Lane Theatre.

•

1894 Polish immigrant Michael Marks and Yorkshireman Tom Spencer opened their Penny Bazaar in Manchester.

•

1924 the first round-the-world flight was completed by aviators from the US Army Air Service.

•

1928 Sir Alexander Fleming discovered penicillin.

•

1928 parliament passed the Dangerous Drugs Act outlawing cannabis.

•

1991 Macmillan Cancer Support held its first World's Biggest Coffee Morning event.

•

1995 Yitzhak Rabin and Yasser Arafat agree on terms giving the West Bank a measure of autonomy.

29 SEPTEMBER

1518 the Venetian painter Tintoretto was born.

•

1829 the Metropolitan Police was founded by a Bill introduced by Sir Robert Peel.

1913 Rudolf Diesel, inventor of the diesel compression ignition engine, disappeared and was presumed drowned in the English Channel.

•

1923 Britain began to govern Palestine under a mandate from the League of Nations.

•

1960 the Russian leader Nikita Khrushchev heckled and thumped his desk during a speech by Harold Macmillan, the prime minister, to the UN general assembly.

•

1979 Pope John Paul II arrived in Ireland for the first papal visit to the country.

1399 King Richard II was deposed by Henry Bolingbroke (King Henry IV).

•

1791 Mozart's *Die Zauberflöte* (*The Magic Flute*) was given its premiere at the Theater auf der Wieden in Vienna.

•

1888 Jack the Ripper's third and fourth victims, Elizabeth Stride and Catherine Eddowes, were killed.

•

1938 after signing the Munich agreement with Adolf Hitler in Germany, Neville Chamberlain returned to Britain and declared that there would be peace in our time.

•

1949 the Berlin Airlift came to an end after 277,264 flights which carried 2,323,738 tons of supplies.

•

1955 actor James Dean died aged 24.

331 BC Alexander the Great conquered the Persian empire by defeating Darius at Gaugamela, near Mosul in modern Iraq.

•

1843 the *News of the World* was first published.

•

1861 Mrs Beeton's *Book of Household Management* was published.

•

1908 Henry Ford's Model T went on sale, with a price tag of $850.

•

1946 the court passed judgement in the Nuremberg trials of leading Nazis.

•

1949 the People's Republic of China was formed with Mao Zedong as its head.

•

1963 the Nuclear Test Ban Treaty, signed by Britain, America and Russia, came into operation.

•

1974 the Watergate trial began.

1608 the first telescope was demonstrated to the States General by Hans Lippershey of the Netherlands.

·

1870 Italy was finally formally unified when, after troops entered Rome, a plebiscite joined it and Lazio to the rest of the kingdom.

·

1901 the first submarine commissioned by the Royal Navy was launched from Barrow.

·

1909 Twickenham staged its first rugby match, between Harlequins and Richmond.

·

1950 Charles Schulz first published *Peanuts*.

·

1950 Legal Aid came into force.

·

1983 Neil Kinnock and Roy Hattersley were elected on a "dream ticket" to lead the Labour Party.

3 OCTOBER

1935 Italy invaded Abyssinia (Ethiopia).

•

1952 the first British atomic bomb was tested off the coast of Australia.

•

1959 postcodes were introduced in Britain.

•

1975 the Spaghetti House siege in Knightsbridge came to an end.

•

1981 a hunger strike by Irish republican prisoners at the Maze prison in Belfast ended after seven months and ten deaths.

•

1990 East and West Germany formally united, ending 45 years of Cold War division.

•

1995 a jury took less than four hours to find OJ Simpson not guilty of murdering his former wife Nicole and a friend of hers, Ron Goodman.

4 OCTOBER

1535 Miles Coverdale's English translation of the Bible was published.

•

1830 the independence of Belgium was proclaimed.

•

1883 the first Orient Express train left Paris for Constantinople.

•

1957 Russia launched the space satellite *Sputnik I*, the first man-made object to leave the Earth's atmsophere.

•

1965 the BBC began broadcasting a TV programme aimed at familiarising Asian immigrants with the British way of life, *Making Yourself at Home*.

•

1970 singer Janis Joplin died of a heroin overdose aged 27.

•

1974 an American, David Kunst, completed the first round-the-world journey on foot, having started the 14,450-mile trip in 1970.

5 OCTOBER

1917 Sir Arthur Lee donated Chequers as a country retreat for prime ministers.

•

1930 the R101 airship crashed near Beauvais, France, killing 47 people.

•

1936 200 men set out on the Jarrow march to London in protest at severe unemployment and poverty in northeast England.

•

1962 starring Sean Connery, the first James Bond film was released — *Dr No*.

•

1964 57 East German refugees escaped to West Berlin after tunnelling under the Berlin Wall — the largest mass escape since the wall was built in 1961.

•

1969 the BBC transmitted the first episode of *Monty Python's Flying Circus*.

6 OCTOBER

1536 William Tyndale, translator of the Bible into English, was burnt at the stake near Brussels.

•

1802 Ludwig van Beethoven wrote the Heiligenstadt Testament.

•

1890 the Mormons in Utah renounced bigamy.

•

1891 Charles Stewart Parnell, champion of Home Rule for Ireland, and according to William Gladstone the most remarkable man of his time, died aged 45.

•

1927 Warner Brothers showed the first feature-length talking film, *The Jazz Singer*, starring Al Jolson, in New York.

•

1981 Anwar Sadat, president of Egypt, was assassinated by Islamic militants at a military parade.

•

1991 Elizabeth Taylor married her eighth husband, Larry Fortensky.

7 OCTOBER

1571 at Lepanto, the Ottoman navy was defeated by that of the Holy League, led by John of Austria.

•

1806 Ralph Wedgwood, nephew of Josiah, patented his invention of carbon paper.

•

1849 Edgar Allan Poe, the first writer to try to live by his pen alone, died aged 40.

•

1919 KLM was founded, making it the oldest airline in the world still operating under its original name.

•

1959 the far side of the moon was first photographed, the pictures being relayed to Earth by Russia's *Lunik III*.

•

2001 the US began Operation Enduring Freedom in Afghanistan.

8 OCTOBER

1085 St Mark's Cathedral, Venice, was consecrated.

•

1871 the Great Fire of Chicago began.

•

1952 112 people were killed at Harrow and Wealdstone
in Britain's deadliest peace time rail disaster.

•

1953 the first London production of *The King and I*
took place.

•

1965 the Post Office Tower opened in London.

•

1982 the musical *Cats* began a record-breaking run
on Broadway which would last for 18 years.

•

1996 PLO president Yasser Arafat paid his first public visit
to Israel for talks with Israeli president Ezer Weizman.

•

2003 film star Arnold Schwarzenegger was elected Governor
of California.

1701 Yale College received its charter.

•

1779 the first Luddite riots, against the introduction of machinery for spinning cotton, began in Manchester.

•

1899 the first petrol-driven motor bus began operating in London.

•

1940 the dome of St Paul's was hit by bombs and the cathedral's altar wrecked during the Luftwaffe's night-time blitz of London.

•

1962 Uganda became independent.

•

1967 Cuban Revolution leader Ernesto "Che" Guevara was shot dead in Bolivia, aged 39.

•

1986 *The Phantom of the Opera*, which would become the second-longest running musical in West End history (after *Les Misérables*), opened at Her Majesty's Theatre.

1903 Emmeline Pankhurst formed the Women's Social and Political Union in Manchester to fight for female emancipation.

•

1935 the first performance of *Porgy and Bess* by George Gershwin took place in New York.

•

1957 a fire at the Windscale facility, Cumbria, became the world's the first nuclear accident.

•

1963 the Nuclear Test Ban Treaty, signed by Britain, America and Russia, came into operation.

•

1975 Richard Burton and Elizabeth Taylor married for the second time.

•

1980 prime minister Margaret Thatcher made a speech at the Conservative Party Conference defending her economic policies: "The lady's not for turning."

1919 the first in-flight meals were served on
a Handley Page flight from London to Paris.

•

1957 the Jodrell Bank radio telescope, designed by
Sir Bernard Lovell, began operating.

•

1967 The Move pop group apologised to prime minister
Harold Wilson for using a nude caricature of him to
promote their record *Flowers in the Rain*.

•

1974 Harold Wilson's Labour government narrowly won
a second term in office.

•

1982 the *Mary Rose*, once Henry VIII's flagship, was raised
from the Solent.

•

1987 a major sonar exploration failed to find any trace
of the Loch Ness monster.

12 OCTOBER

1492 Christopher Columbus discovered the New World, landing on Guanahani, an island in the Bahamas. (San Salvador is the name Columbus gave the island.)

•

1928 the iron lung was used for the first time, in Boston, Massachusetts.

•

1979 Douglas Adams published *The Hitchhiker's Guide to the Galaxy*.

•

1984 five people were killed when an IRA bomb exploded at the Grand Hotel in Brighton, East Sussex, during the Conservative Party conference.

•

1997 singer John Denver died aged 53 when his light aircraft crashed off California.

•

1999 the UN celebrated the birth of the world's six billionth person, symbolically honouring a baby in Sarajevo.

13 OCTOBER

54 the Roman emperor Claudius died, reputedly poisoned
with mushrooms by his wife Agrippina.

•

1792 the cornerstone of the White House was laid by
George Washington.

•

1884 Greenwich was adopted as the prime meridian
at a conference in Washington DC.

•

1988 the Turin Shroud, revered by many Christians as
Christ's burial cloth, was declared, after carbon-dating tests,
to date from the Middle Ages.

•

1997 Tony Blair met the Sinn Fein leader Gerry Adams,
the first meeting between a British prime minister and
a Northern Irish republican leader for 70 years.

1066 the Battle of Hastings was fought at Senlac Hill.

1939 HMS *Royal Oak* was sunk by a U-boat in Scapa Flow.

1944 Field Marshal Erwin Rommel committed suicide.

1946 Chuck Yeager became the first pilot to fly faster than the speed of sound.

1964 the Nobel Peace Prize was awarded to Martin Luther King Jr.

1983 Cecil Parkinson resigned as trade secretary after revelations about an extra-marital affair.

1994 Israeli prime minister Yitzhak Rabin, foreign minister Shimon Peres and Palestine Liberation Organisation chairman Yasser Arafat shared the Nobel Peace Prize.

15 OCTOBER

1783 a tethered hot-air balloon constructed by the Montgolfier Brothers made, to a height of 80ft, the first public ascent while carrying a person, Pilâtre de Rozier.

•

1894 French army officer Alfred Dreyfus was arrested on a charge of treason.

•

1928 the airship *Graf Zeppelin* landed in New Jersey after its first transatlantic crossing.

•

1956 the first modern computer programming language, Fortran, appeared.

•

1964 Leonid Brezhnev replaced Nikita Khrushchev as general secretary of the Communist Party in Russia.

•

1997 the Thrust supersonic car broke the sound barrier on land for the first time, reaching 764.168mph.

16 OCTOBER

1793 Marie Antoinette, former Queen of France, was guillotined, aged 37.

•

1834 the medieval Palace of Westminster, which housed the House of Commons, burnt down when sticks used to tally the Exchequer's accounts caught fire.

•

1847 *Jane Eyre* by Charlotte Brontë was published.

•

1908 Samuel Cody made the first successful aeroplane flight in Britain.

•

1964 Harold Wilson became prime minister for the first time.

•

1978 Cardinal Karol Wojtyla, Archbishop of Cracow, became Pope John Paul II — the first non-Italian pontiff for 450 years.

•

1987 southern England was unexpectedly battered by hurricane-force winds, which killed 18 people and toppled 15 million trees.

1651 Charles II fled to France after his defeat at Worcester.

•

1739 the UK's first dedicated children's charity,
The Foundling Hospital (now Coram) was created
by royal charter.

•

1814 eight people died when 323,000 gallons of beer
flooded streets around Tottenham Court Road, London.

•

1956 the Queen opened Calder Hall, Britain's first nuclear
power station.

•

1973 Arab oil producers increased prices and cut back
production in response to US support of Israel in the
Yom Kippur War.

•

1998 the former Chilean dictator, Augusto Pinochet, was
arrested in London after an extradition request from Spain.

18 OCTOBER

1016 the Danes defeated the Saxons at the
Battle of Assandun.

•

1685 Louis XIV revoked the Edict of Nantes to deprive
French Protestants of their liberties.

•

1867 Alaska officially became part of the United States
with the exchange of the ratified treaty at Sitka.

•

1922 the British Broadcasting Company was formed
(later the British Broadcasting Corporation).

•

1963 Sir Alec Douglas-Home became the prime minister
after winning the fiercely fought Conservative Party
leadership contest.

•

1989 Erich Honecker, East Germany's leader, was forced
to resign as popular discontent mounted.

•

1995 the racehorse Red Rum, three times winner of the
Grand National, died aged 30.

19 OCTOBER

1813 Napoleon was defeated by the Allies at the Battle of
Leipzig in Saxony.

•

1914 the first Battle of Ypres began.

•

1960 the US State Department embargoed the shipment
to Cuba of all goods except medicine and food.

•

1970 British Petroleum announced it had struck oil
in the UK's sector of the North Sea.

•

1987 Black Monday occurred when the Dow Jones
Industrial Average plunged a record 508 points,
or 22.6 per cent.

•

1989 the murder convictions of the Guildford Four,
jailed since 1975 for IRA bomb attacks, were quashed.

20 OCTOBER

1818 the western border between Canada and the United States was defined as a line from the farthest northwest part of Lake of the Woods to the 49th parallel and thence west to the Rocky Mountains.

•

1842 Grace Darling, heroine of the wreck of the *Forfarshire*, died of tuberculosis aged 26.

•

1960 the obscenity trial against Penguin Books, publishers of *Lady Chatterley's Lover*, began in London with jurors being handed copies of the unexpurgated edition.

•

1968 Jackie Kennedy married Aristotle Onassis.

•

1973 Sydney Opera House opened.

•

2011 President Gaddafi was killed by rebel forces in Libya.

1805 the British defeated a Franco-Spanish fleet at the Battle of Trafalgar, with the loss in action of Admiral Lord Nelson.

•

1944 the first German city, Aachen, fell to the Americans.

1960 the US presidential candidates John F Kennedy and Richard M Nixon took part in their fourth and final presidential debate.

•

1966 a coal slag heap engulfed a school and houses in Aberfan, near Merthyr Tydfil, killing 144 people, including 116 children.

•

1969 Willy Brandt was elected chancellor of West Germany.

•

1981 socialist Andreas Papandreou became Greece's first non-conservative premier for 50 years.

451 the Council of Chalcedon drafted a creed defining Jesus's divinity.

•

1746 Princeton University received its royal charter.

•

1797 the first parachute jump was made by André-Jacques Garnerin from a balloon several thousand feet above the Parc Monceau, Paris.

•

1938 the American physicist Chester F Carlson made the first photocopied image.

•

1962 President Kennedy announced that the US was placing Cuba under naval blockade until the Soviet Union removed ballistic missile sites from the island.

•

1962 Nelson Mandela pleaded not guilty at the start of his treason trial in South Africa.

42 BC three weeks after Cassius met the same fate, Brutus committed suicide after being defeated by Mark Antony and Octavian at Philippi, Macedonia.

•

1642 Royalists and Parliamentarians clashed at the Battle of Edgehill, with both sides later claiming victory.

•

1707 the first parliament of Great Britain met.

•

1942 the Second Battle of El Alamein began.

•

1956 an uprising against Soviet rule began in Hungary.

•

1980 the Soviet prime minister Alexei Kosygin resigned, due to illness.

•

1983 300 US Marines and French troops were killed when suicide bombers attacked barracks in Beirut.

1604 King James VI of Scotland was proclaimed James I, King of England, Scotland, France and Ireland.

•

1851 British astronomer William Lassell discovered Ariel and Umbriel, two moons of Uranus.

•

1929 on what became known as Black Thursday, panic selling began in earnest on the New York Stock Exchange, leading to the Wall Street Crash five days later.

•

1945 the United Nations was formally established.

•

1964 Northern Rhodesia became the independent republic of Zambia, with Kenneth Kaunda its first president.

•

2004 after a record 49 matches unbeaten in the Premier League, Arsenal lost to Manchester United.

1415 English bowmen secured the defeat of a French army at the Battle of Agincourt.

•

1760 King George III ascended the throne.

1854 the Charge of the Light Brigade took place during the Battle of Balaclava in the Crimean War.

•

1924 the bogus Zinoviev Letter, purporting to encourage British Communists to engage in sedition, was published in the *Daily Mail*.

•

1929 reputedly while working a night shift at a power station, William Faulkner began writing the novel *As I Lay Dying*.

•

1976 the new National Theatre building was opened.

•

1983 the US invaded Grenada following the assassination of premier Maurice Bishop.

26 OCTOBER

899 Alfred the Great died aged 50.

•

1881 a gunfight took place at the OK Corral, Tombstone, Arizona, between Doc Holliday and Wyatt, Virgil and Morgan Earp and the Clantons and McLaurys.

1907 the Territorial Army was founded.

•

1951 Winston Churchill became prime minister again after a narrow election win.

•

1965 the four Beatles were each invested MBE at Buckingham Palace.

•

1986 Jeffrey Archer resigned as deputy chairman of the Conservative Party.

•

2000 Lord Phillips issued his report into the spread of BSE and variant CJD, criticising scientists and government ministers.

27 OCTOBER

1644 the English Civil War's second, and again inconclusive, Battle of Newbury took place.

•

1904 the New York subway opened to the public.

•

1925 the American inventor Fred Waller patented the first water skis, called Dolphin Akwa-Skees.

•

1968 an estimated 6,000 marchers, protesting against US involvement in Vietnam, confronted police outside the US Embassy in London.

•

1971 the Democratic Republic of the Congo was renamed Zaïre.

•

1977 former Liberal Party leader Jeremy Thorpe denied conspiring to have his homosexual lover murdered.

•

1986 the London Stock Exchange's Big Bang took place, transforming the way shares were traded.

28 OCTOBER

1726 Jonathan Swift's *Gulliver's Travels* was published anonymously.

•

1929 Black Monday occurred during the Wall Street stock market crash.

•

1956 Elvis Presley was vaccinated against polio on television and within six months, levels of immunisation in the US rose from less than 1 per cent to 80 per cent.

•

1957 the BBC news and current affairs programme *Today* aired on the Home Service for the first time.

•

1958 Angelo Giuseppe Roncalli became Pope John XXIII.

•

1958 the State Opening of Parliament and the Queen's Speech were televised for the first time.

•

1971 MPs voted in favour of Britain joining the European Economic Community.

1787 Mozart's opera Don Giovanni was first performed in Prague.

•

1863 the International Committee for the Relief of the Wounded (later to be known as the International Red Cross and Red Crescent Movement) was founded.

•

1901 the Royal Aero Club of the United Kingdom, the national co-ordinating body for air sport, was formed.

•

1927 the Tomb of Genghis Khan was discovered by the Russian archaeologist Peter Kozlov.

•

1929 the Depression began after the collapse of the New York Stock Exchange.

•

1964 Tanganyika and Zanzibar united to become Tanzania.

•

1986 the M25 motorway was opened.

30 OCTOBER

1485 the Yeomen of the Guard, more commonly known as the Beefeaters, was founded by King Henry VII.

•

1918 the Ottoman Turks signed the Armistice of Mondros, ending their involvement in the First World War.

•

1922 Mussolini's fascist government was formed in Rome.

•

1938 Orson Welles's production on US radio of HG Wells's *The War of the Worlds* panicked listeners who believed its story of a Martian invasion to be true.

•

1957 the government revealed plans for a Life Peerages Act, which would, for the first time, allow women to sit in the House of Lords.

31 OCTOBER

1815 Sir Humphrey Davy patented the miner's safety lamp.

•

1888 pneumatic bicycle tyres were patented by
John Boyd Dunlop.

1933 the carving of the heads of four US presidents on
Mount Rushmore in South Dakota was completed.

•

1951 Britain's first zebra crossings were introduced.

•

1955 it was announced that Princess Margaret had decided
not to marry Group Captain Peter Townsend.

•

1964 the Windmill Theatre in London — famous for its
risqué revues — closed.

•

1984 Indira Ghandi was assassinated by two Sikh
bodyguards.

•

2011 the global population reached seven billion.

1 NOVEMBER

1512 the ceiling of the Sistine Chapel, painted by Michelangelo, was exhibited to the public for the first time.

·

1695 the Bank of Scotland was founded.

·

1755 an earthquake and tsunami destroyed Lisbon, killing more than 60,000 people.

·

1922 the radio licence fee (initially ten shillings) was introduced in Britain.

·

1952 the United States detonated the first hydrogen bomb at Eniwetok atoll in the Pacific Ocean.

·

1956 Premium Savings Bonds were launched by Harold Macmillan, chancellor of the exchequer.

·

1959 the first stretch of the M1 opened between junctions 5 at Watford and 18 Crick/Rugby.

·

1993 the Maastricht Treaty came into effect.

2 NOVEMBER

1903 the *Daily Mirror* was first published.

•

1917 the Balfour Declaration conveyed the British government's approval of establishing a Jewish homeland in Palestine.

•

1936 the world's first regular high-definition television service began with a BBC broadcast from Alexandra Palace, London.

•

1947 Howard Hughes's flying boat, nicknamed "The Spruce Goose", the largest aircraft ever constructed, made its only flight.

•

1960 Penguin Books was acquitted of obscenity in publishing *Lady Chatterley's Lover*.

•

1964 in an internal coup in Saudi Arabia, King Saud was replaced by his brother Faisal.

3 NOVEMBER

1534 England's parliament passed the Act of Supremacy making King Henry VIII head of the church.

•

1706 an earthquake in the Abruzzo region of Italy killed 2,500 people.

•

1793 feminist writer Olympe de Gouges was guillotined, aged 45.

•

1926 Annie Oakley, theatrical performer who wowed crowds with her dead-shot markmanship, died in Greenville, Ohio, aged 66.

•

1936 Franklin D Roosevelt was re-elected US president.

•

1957 Laika, a Russian dog, was sent into space in *Sputnik II.*

•

1964 Lyndon B Johnson was elected president, having held the office since the assassination of President Kennedy.

4 NOVEMBER

1843 a two-day operation to haul the statue of Nelson to the top of the 170ft column in Trafalgar Square was completed.

•

1918 poet Wilfred Owen was killed, aged 25.

•

1922 Howard Carter found the entrance to the tomb of Tutankhamun.

•

1956 Soviet tanks crushed the Hungarian Uprising.

•

1966 flooding of the Arno in Florence destroyed numerous works of art.

•

1979 Iranian students stormed the US embassy in Tehran, taking many hostages.

•

1980 Ronald Reagan was elected the 40th US president.

•

1992 Bill Clinton was elected the 42nd US president.

•

2008 Barack Obama became the first US president of African-American descent.

5 NOVEMBER

1605 the Gunpowder Plot was foiled and Guy Fawkes was arrested.

•

1854 French and British forces defeated the Russians at the Battle of Inkerman, in the Crimean War.

•

1909 the first Woolworths store in Britain opened in Church Street, Liverpool.

•

1914 Britain declared war on Turkey and annexed Cyprus.

•

1956 British and French paratroops landed near Port Said, Egypt, during the Suez Crisis.

•

1967 49 people were killed in the Hither Green rail disaster.

•

1991 newspaper publisher Robert Maxwell disappeared from his yacht *Lady Ghislaine* off Tenerife.

•

2006 former ruler of Iraq Saddam Hussein was sentenced to death.

6 NOVEMBER

1429 the seven-year-old Henry VI was crowned
King of England.

•

1860 Abraham Lincoln was elected the 16th president
of the United States (1861–65).

•

1932 in Germany's last election before Hitler came to
power, the Nazi Party lost 34 Reichstag seats and 2 million
voters on a reduced turn-out of electors.

•

1986 45 people, many of them oil workers, were killed in
the deadliest civilian helicopter crash on record when their
Chinook came down at Sumburgh, in the Shetlands.

•

1999 Australians voted in a referendum to reject replacing
the Queen as head of state.

7 NOVEMBER

1783 John Austin was the last convict hanged at London's Tyburn.

•

1872 the brig *Mary Celeste* left New York for Genoa, to be found a month later, sailing in the North Atlantic in perfect condition but with no one on board.

•

1917 the October Revolution (so called because this day was October 25 by the old-style calendar) began in Petrograd, Russia.

•

1956 the UN general assembly called on the UK, France and Israel to withdraw their troops from Egypt.

•

2000 Hillary Clinton won a seat in the Senate — the first First Lady to win elective office.

8 NOVEMBER

1602 the Bodleian Library in Oxford opened.

•

1895 the physicist Wilhelm Röntgen discovered X-rays during an electrical experiment at Würzburg University.

•

1960 John F Kennedy was elected the 35th US president.

•

1987 a bomb killed 11 people at a Remembrance Day service in Enniskillen, Northern Ireland.

•

1990 Mary Robinson was elected Ireland's first woman president.

•

1997 the main channel of China's Yangtze River began to be blocked in preparation for the world's largest hydroelectric power project.

•

2004 10,000 US troops laid siege to insurgents in the Iraqi city of Fallujah.

9 NOVEMBER

1859 flogging in the British Army was abolished.

•

1888 the body of Jack the Ripper's fifth and last known victim, 25-year-old Mary Jane Kelly, was found in Whitechapel, London.

•

1918 the abdication of Kaiser Wilhelm II, German Emperor 1888–1918, was announced.

•

1938 Kristallnacht (the Night of Broken Glass) took place in Nazi Germany.

•

1953 Dylan Thomas died aged 39.

•

1970 Charles de Gaulle died of a heart attack aged 79.

•

1976 the UN general assembly adopted a programme of action against apartheid in South Africa.

•

1989 the demolition of the Berlin Wall began.

1820 the Bill of Pains and Penalties, by which King George IV hoped to deprive Queen Caroline of her titles and dissolve their marriage, was withdrawn by the government.

•

1852 Gideon Mantell, geologist who discovered fossil bones of the iguanodon in the Sussex Weald, died.

1871 Henry Morton Stanley met Dr David Livingstone at Ujiji, Tanganyika.

•

1908 the Reichstag debated unhelpful comments by Kaiser Wilhelm II about anti-British feeling in Germany, which had been quoted in a *Daily Telegraph* article.

•

1982 Leonid Brezhnev, general secretary of the Soviet Communist Party 1964–82, died.

1880 Ned Kelly, Australian outlaw, was hanged, aged 25.

1919 Britain commemorated the first anniversary
of Armistice Day with the first two-minute silence.

1940 British naval air forces crippled the Italian fleet
at Taranto.

1953 the BBC television programme *Panorama* was
first broadcast.

1965 Ian Smith, the Rhodesian prime minister, issued
his country's unilateral declaration of independence from
Britain.

1992 the Church of England voted to allow women
to become priests.

2000 155 people died in a fire on a funicular railway
in the Austrian Alps.

2004 Yasser Arafat, who had led the Palestinians for
40 years, died.

12 NOVEMBER

1912 a search party discovered the bodies of Captain Robert Scott and other members of his expedition, who had died eight months earlier when returning from the South Pole.

•

1944 RAF bombers sank the German battleship *Tirpitz* in Tromso fjord, Norway.

•

1954 Ellis Island, which had processed immigrants to the US since 1892, closed.

•

1969 Aleksandr Solzhenitsyn was expelled from the Soviet Writers' Union for antisocial behaviour.

•

1974 the first salmon to be discovered in the Thames since 1833 was retrieved from the filters of West Thurrock power station.

13 NOVEMBER

1002 the St Brice's Day Massacre took place, after King Ethelred II's edict to slaughter all Danes.

•

1887 the Social Democratic Federation's demonstration in Trafalgar Square was dispersed by police, causing more than 100 casualties in the first so-called Bloody Sunday.

•

1945 Charles de Gaulle was elected president of the French provisional government at the end of the Second World War.

•

1965 the F-word was used for the first time on BBC television, by drama critic Kenneth Tynan during a live discussion on censorship.

•

2015 130 people were killed in linked terrorist attacks in Paris.

14 NOVEMBER

1608 an entry was made in the Stationers' Register for George Chapman's edition of Homer.

•

1715 a Jacobite army surrendered at Preston.

•

1851 Herman Melville published *Moby Dick*.

•

1889 US journalist Nellie Bly set off to travel around the world in 80 days, and did so in 72.

•

1896 the speed limit for horseless carriages in Britain was raised to 14mph.

•

1940 Coventry Cathedral was virtually destroyed by German bombing.

•

1952 the *New Musical Express* launched its popular-music chart.

•

1973 Princess Anne and Captain Mark Phillips were married in Westminster Abbey.

15 NOVEMBER

1889 Brazil became a republic.

•

1899 the US steamship *St Paul*, en route to England,
was the first ship to receive radio messages, transmitted
from the Needles off the Isle of Wight.

•

1923 German inflation reached a peak with the currency
standing at four trillion marks to the dollar.

•

1979 Margaret Thatcher named Anthony Blunt
as a spy for the Russians and the fourth man in the
Burgess-Philby-Maclean spy ring.

•

1985 the Anglo-Irish agreement was signed at
Hillsborough Castle.

•

2007 Cyclone Sidr hit the southwest coast of Bangladesh,
killing more than 5,000 people.

16 NOVEMBER

42 BC Tiberius, second Roman emperor AD 14–37, was born in Rome.

●

1724 the highwayman Jack Sheppard was hanged at Tyburn, London.

●

1855 the Scottish explorer David Livingstone first saw, and named after his monarch, the spectacular Victoria Falls on what is now the Zimbabwe/Zambia border.

●

1857 24 Victoria Crosses were won in a single day at the relief of Lucknow, India.

●

1899 Charles Wyndham opened the Wyndham's Theatre in Charing Cross Road, London.

●

1920 the Queensland and Northern Territory Aerial Services airline was founded: Qantas.

●

1965 the Soviet Union launched *Venus 3,* an unmanned spacecraft that crash-landed on Venus.

17 NOVEMBER

9 Vespasian, Roman emperor in whose reign the building of the Colosseum was started, was born in Italy.

•

1869 the Suez Canal was officially opened to navigation.

•

1919 Sylvia Beach opened her bookshop and library, Shakespeare and Company, on the Left Bank in Paris.

•

1968 Mervyn Peake, novelist and illustrator, died aged 57.

•

1970 a US patent was issued to Doug Engelbart for his invention of the computer mouse, so called because of its tail-like cable.

•

1993 judges from 11 nations were sworn in at the inaugural session of the UN's Yugoslavia War Crimes Tribunal.

18 NOVEMBER

1095 the Council of Clermont began, leading to the First Crusade.

•

1477 William Caxton issued *The Dictes or Sayengis of the Philosophres*, the first book printed at his Westminster press.

•

1626 the new St Peter's Church in Rome was consecrated.

•

1852 the state funeral of the Duke of Wellington took place.

•

1916 the Battle of the Somme, which had begun on July 1, ended.

•

1987 a fire at King's Cross on the London Underground killed 31 people.

•

1991 after four years as a hostage, Terry Waite was released by the Islamic Jihad for the Liberation of Palestine.

1703 The Man in the Iron Mask, a prisoner in the Bastille who was immortalised by Alexandre Dumas but whose true identity was never revealed, died.

•

1850 Alfred, Lord Tennyson, became poet laureate in succession to Wordsworth.

1863 US president Abraham Lincoln delivered his Gettysburg Address.

•

1949 Prince Rainier III was crowned ruler of Monaco.

•

1969 the second Apollo mission landed on the moon as part of the Ocean of Storms mission.

•

1994 Britain's first National Lottery draw took place.

•

1998 in the Lewinsky affair, hearings began as to whether President Clinton should be impeached.

20 NOVEMBER

1906 Charles Stewart Rolls and Frederick Henry Royce founded Rolls-Royce.

•

1945 the Nuremberg war crimes trials began.

1947 Princess Elizabeth and the newly created Duke of Edinburgh were married in Westminster Abbey.

•

1951 Snowdonia was designated a national park.

•

1962 President John F Kennedy announced the lifting of the US naval blockade on Cuba.

•

1992 fire swept through Windsor Castle, causing extensive damage.

•

1995 The Princess of Wales spoke openly about her troubled marriage in a television interview with the BBC, watched by a record audience.

1783 in Paris, Pilâtre de Rozier and the Marquis d'Arlandes made the first manned, untethered hot-air balloon flight.

•

1918 ten days after the end of the First World War, the British interned 74 ships of the German High Seas Fleet in Scapa Flow, Orkney.

•

1953 experts at the Natural History Museum in London declared the skull of the Piltdown Man a forgery.

•

1974 two bombs exploded in central Birmingham pubs, killing 21 people and injuring more than 180.

•

1995 a US-brokered peace agreement, signed at Dayton, Ohio, ended the war in Bosnia-Herzegovina.

1916 writer Jack London died aged 40.

•

1946 the first Biro ballpoint pens went on sale in Britain.

•

1963 President John F Kennedy was shot dead
in Dallas, Texas.

•

1963 authors Aldous Huxley and CS Lewis died.

•

1975 King Juan Carlos acceded to the Spanish throne.

•

1997 Australian singer Michael Hutchence died aged 37.

•

2003 England won the Rugby World Cup with a last-minute
drop-kick by Jonny Wilkinson.

•

2004 the Orange Revolution began in Ukraine.

•

2012 a ceasefire began in the Gaza Strip after 150 deaths
in eight days.

23 NOVEMBER

1852 Britain's first pillar boxes were introduced
in St Helier, Jersey.

•

1863 during the American Civil War, the Battle of
Chattanooga began.

1874 the first edition of *Far From the Madding Crowd*
by Thomas Hardy was published.

•

1936 the first edition of *Life* magazine appeared.

•

1955 the British government handed over the
administration of the Cocos Islands in the Indian Ocean
to Australia.

•

1963 the first episode of *Doctor Who* was screened
by the BBC.

•

1984 almost 1,000 passengers were trapped in the
London Underground after a fire broke out at Oxford
Circus station.

24 NOVEMBER

1642 Abel Tasman discovered Van Diemen's Land,
later renamed Tasmania.

·

1859 Charles Darwin published *On the Origin of Species*.

·

1877 Anna Sewell published *Black Beauty*.

·

1954 the first US presidential aeroplane to be christened
Air Force One was named.

·

1962 the first episode of the satirical programme
That Was The Week That Was was broadcast.

·

1963 Lee Harvey Oswald, charged with the assassination
of President John F Kennedy, was shot dead by Jack Ruby
in Texas.

·

1991 singer Freddie Mercury died aged 45.

·

2012 a fire at a clothes factory in Bangladesh killed
112 people.

1120 William, King Henry I's heir, drowned in the English Channel, leading to a struggle for the throne between his sister Matilda and cousin Stephen.

•

1882 the first night of Gilbert and Sullivan's *Iolanthe* took place at the Savoy Theatre, London.

•

1952 Agatha Christie's *The Mousetrap* opened at the Ambassadors Theatre, London.

•

1956 Miss Rose Heilbron, QC, was the first woman lawyer to be appointed a recorder.

•

1974 singer-songwriter Nick Drake died aged 26.

•

1995 the result of an Irish referendum was announced, with 50.2 per cent voting for the legalisation of divorce.

1703 about 8,000 people died during Britain's Great Storm.

•

1789 the newly elected first president of America George Washington proclaimed this day Thanksgiving Day, which is now observed on the fourth Thursday of each November.

•

1914 nearly 800 were killed in an accidental explosion on the battleship HMS *Bulwark* in the Medway.

•

1983 gold bullion worth £25 million was stolen from the Brinks-Mat security warehouse at Heathrow airport.

•

2000 George W Bush was certified the winner of Florida's decisive 25 electoral-college votes, and next day declared himself to have won the US presidential election.

1914 two policewomen, the first to be granted official status in Britain, reported for duty in Grantham, Lincolnshire.

•

1936 it was reported that Italy would enter the German-Japanese pact against communism.

•

1942 with the German army occupying Toulon, the French navy scuttled its fleet that was anchored there.

•

1967 President Charles de Gaulle said that he was not prepared to begin negotiations for Britain's entry to the Common Market.

•

1975 author Ross McWhirter was murdered by the IRA.

•

1990 John Major won the Conservative Party's leadership election, and became prime minister the next day.

1660 a meeting of 12 scholars, including Christopher Wren, decided to set up a College for the Promoting of Physico-Mathematicall Experimentall Learning, which became the Royal Society.

•

1814 *The Times* became the first newspaper printed on a steam-powered press.

•

1919 Nancy, Viscountess Astor, won a by-election in Plymouth, becoming the first female MP to sit in the House of Commons.

•

1943 Churchill, Roosevelt and Stalin met in Tehran to discuss their combined strategy for defeating the Germans.

•

1990 Margaret Thatcher formally tendered her resignation as prime minister and left 10 Downing Street for the last time.

29 NOVEMBER

1877 Thomas Edison demonstrated his hand-cranked phonograph, which recorded sound onto cylinders.

•

1907 King Edward VII appointed Florence Nightingale to the Order of Merit.

•

1929 an aircraft navigated by the US explorer Richard E Byrd made the first flight over the South Pole.

•

1945 Yugoslavia was proclaimed a Federal People's Republic.

•

1947 the UN voted to partition Palestine into a Jewish state and an Arab state, with Jerusalem internationally administered.

•

1968 demonstrators staged a sit-in at the BBC's new studios in Cardiff, protesting at the shortage of Welsh-speaking programmes.

1678 Roman Catholics were banned from the
English parliament.

•

1872 the first international football match took place, with
Scotland and England drawing 0–0 in Partick, Glasgow.

•

1936 Crystal Palace, built for the Great Exhibition of 1851,
and moved from Hyde Park to Sydenham in southeast
London in 1854, was destroyed by fire.

•

1968 the Trade Descriptions Act came into force.

•

1982 Michael Jackson released *Thriller*, which became
the best-selling album in history.

•

1995 Bill Clinton became the first US president to visit
Northern Ireland, touring Belfast and Londonderry (Derry).

1 DECEMBER

1913 the world's first moving assembly line was opened by carmakers Ford.

•

1942 the Beveridge report on social security was published, heralding Britain's welfare state.

•

1955 an African-American, Rosa Parks, was arrested in Alabama for refusing to give up her bus seat to a white man.

•

1990 British and French workers finished digging the Channel Tunnel, joining the UK to the Continent for the first time since the Ice Age.

•

1995 the former Barings Bank trader Nick Leeson pleaded guilty to fraud related to losses that broke the bank.

2 DECEMBER

1697 the quire, the first part of Christopher Wren's
St Paul's Cathedral to be finished, opened.

•

1793 the poet Samuel Taylor Coleridge enlisted in the
15th Light Dragoons.

•

1804 Napoleon Bonaparte crowned himself French
emperor in Paris.

•

1805 Napoleon used a blanket of fog to shatter a larger
Russo-Austrian army at the Battle of Austerlitz, in Moravia.

•

1852 the nephew of Emperor Napoleon I took the title
Napoleon III.

•

1942 in Chicago, a team led by Enrico Fermi created
the first controlled nuclear chain reaction.

•

1971 six states formed the independent
United Arab Emirates.

3 DECEMBER

1910 neon lighting developed by Frenchman
Georges Claude was displayed for the first time
at the Paris Motor Show.

•

1926 Agatha Christie disappeared from her home,
to be found the following week staying in a hotel,
claiming loss of memory.

•

1944 Britain's Home Guard was officially stood down.

•

1967 Christiaan Barnard carried out the world's first
heart transplant at Groote Schuur Hospital, Cape Town.

•

1984 an escape of toxic gas from the Union Carbide
pesticide plant near Bhopal, India, killed several
thousand people.

•

1993 Diana, Princess of Wales, announced her withdrawal
from public life.

4 DECEMBER

1791 *The Observer* was first published.

•

1829 the British in India outlawed the Hindu practice of suttee, the self-immolation of widows on their husband's funeral pyres.

•

1956 Jerry Lee Lewis, Carl Perkins, Johnny Cash and Elvis Presley recorded a jam session, not released until 1981.

•

1957 the Lewisham rail crash, in which 89 people died, occurred in southeast London.

•

1988 Edwina Currie, under-secretary of state for health, sparked controversy by claiming that most British eggs produced were infected by salmonella.

•

1991 Pan Am, formerly the world's largest airline, went out of business after 64 years.

5 DECEMBER

1766 James Christie held his first auction in London.

•

1872 the brig *Mary Celeste* was found drifting in the Atlantic.

•

1933 Prohibition was repealed in America after 14 years.

•

1934 the first meeting took place of the British Council, then known as the British Committee for Relations with Other Countries.

•

1952 the Great Smog began in London, four days of extreme air pollution which caused 10,000 deaths.

•

1958 the Preston Bypass, Britain's first stretch of motorway, was opened.

•

1974 the last episode of *Monty Python's Flying Circus* was televised by the BBC.

6 DECEMBER

1917 at Halifax, Nova Scotia, 2,000 people died when
the largest man-made explosion to date occurred after
a French munitions ship caught fire.

•

1917 following the Bolshevik Revolution, Finland declared
its independence from Russia.

•

1922 the Irish Free State was proclaimed.

•

1943 British forces in Italy captured Monte Camino,
dominating the approach to Cassino.

•

1975 the six-day Balcombe Street siege began in London
when four IRA gunmen took a middle-aged couple hostage.

•

1988 singer Roy Orbison died aged 52.

•

1991 Dubrovnik, in Croatia, was bombarded during
its siege by Serb-led Yugoslav forces.

7 DECEMBER

1732 the Theatre Royal, Covent Garden (now the Royal Opera House), opened.

1787 Delaware became the first state to ratify the federal constitution of America.

1875 a German steamer, the *Deutschland*, sank off the Kent coast, inspiring Gerard Manley Hopkins's poem *The Wreck of the Deutschland*.

1941 Japanese aircraft attacked the main base of the US Pacific Fleet at Pearl Harbor.

1955 Clement Attlee stepped down as Labour leader.

1988 an earthquake in Armenia killed more than 25,000 people.

8 DECEMBER

1854 Pope Pius IX declared the Immaculate Conception of the Virgin Mary to be an article of faith.

·

1864 Isambard Kingdom Brunel's Clifton Suspension Bridge was opened five years after its engineer's death at the age of 53 through overwork and 40 cigars a day.

·

1941 the US and Britain declared war on Japan.

·

1980 the former Beatle John Lennon was shot dead in New York aged 40.

·

1981 Arthur Scargill was elected president of the National Union of Mineworkers.

·

1987 Ronald Reagan and Mikhail Gorbachev agreed to reduce their nations' nuclear arsenals.

9 DECEMBER

1688 the defeat of his forces by those of William of Orange at the Battle of Reading led King James II to flee England.

•

1854 Alfred, Lord Tennyson's Crimean War poem *The Charge of the Light Brigade* was published in *The London Examiner*.

•

1905 the premiere of Richard Strauss's opera *Salome* was held in Dresden.

•

1960 the first episode of *Coronation Street* was screened.

•

1979 smallpox became the first disease to be eradicated by man.

•

1990 Lech Walesa, who in 1983 had received the Nobel Peace Prize, was elected president of Poland.

10 DECEMBER

1845 the civil engineer Robert Thompson patented pneumatic tyres.

•

1868 the world's first traffic lights, off London's Parliament Square, began operating.

•

1898 Cuba became an independent state.

•

1902 the original Aswan Dam, built by the British to control the Nile flood, was completed.

•

1907 in London, more than 1,000 medical students battled police officers in riots over experiments on animals.

•

1909 the Swedish writer Selma Lagerlöf (*The Wonderful Adventures of Nils*) became the first woman awarded the Nobel Prize for Literature.

•

1936 Edward VIII abdicated in order to marry the American divorcée Wallis Simpson.

11 DECEMBER

1946 the UN International Children's Emergency Fund was created to provide relief to children in war-torn countries.

•

1967 a prototype Concorde went on show for the first time, in Toulouse.

•

1972 the Apollo 17 mission became the last to land astronauts on the moon.

•

1998 the $327.6 million Mars Climate Orbiter was launched from Cape Caneveral — it would later be lost because one of the ground teams was using imperial units and another was using metric.

•

2008 US stockbroker Bernie Madoff was arrested and later charged with defrauding clients of $64 billion.

12 DECEMBER

1896 Guglielmo Marconi gave the first public demonstration of radio at Toynbee Hall, east London.

•

1913 an Italian, Vincenzo Perugia, was arrested and charged with stealing the *Mona Lisa* from the Louvre in Paris three years previously.

•

1940 Sheffield was blitzed by the Luftwaffe, and again three nights later, killing 660 people.

•

1955 Christopher Cockerell patented his prototype of the hovercraft.

•

1964 Kenya became a republic within the Commonwealth.

•

1969 bombs planted by terrorists exploded in Rome and Milan, claiming 27 lives.

•

1988 35 people were killed in a rail crash at Clapham Junction, south London.

13 DECEMBER

1577 Francis Drake set sail from Plymouth on the *Pelican* (later renamed the *Golden Hind*) on the first circumnavigation of the globe by an Englishman.

•

1642 the Dutch explorer Abel Tasman first sighted New Zealand.

1862 Confederate forces under Robert E Lee won the Battle of Fredericksburg in the American Civil War.

•

1937 the Japanese army occupied the Chinese city of Nanking.

•

1974 Malta was proclaimed a republic within the British Commonwealth.

•

1981 martial law was declared in Poland by its leader General Wojciech Jaruzelski in an effort to stifle the activities of Solidarity.

•

1983 the novelist Mary Renault died.

14 DECEMBER

1900 Professor Max Planck revealed his revolutionary ideas on quantum physics at a meeting of the German Physics Society.

•

1911 Roald Amundsen reached the South Pole.

•

1918 at the general election, women over 30 were for the first time entitled to vote.

•

1946 the UN general assembly voted to establish the UN headquarters in New York.

•

1955 Hugh Gaitskell was elected leader of the Labour Party.

•

2003 the former leader of Iraq Saddam Hussein was captured after evading capture for eight months.

15 DECEMBER

1890 Sitting Bull was killed in South Dakota.

•

1893 Dvorak's 9th Symphony, *From the New World*,
received its first hearing at Carnegie Hall in New York.

1930 Australian cricketer Don Bradman, aged 22,
took his first Test wicket (Ivan Barrow, West Indies, lbw).

•

1939 nylon yarn was first produced commercially
in Delaware, US.

•

1964 the Canadian parliament voted in favour of a single
maple-leaf design for its national flag.

•

1982 the 13-year Spanish blockade of Gibraltar was lifted.

•

1993 the British and Irish prime ministers, John Major and
Albert Reynolds, signed the Joint Declaration on Peace.

16 DECEMBER

1431 the ten-year-old King Henry VI of England was crowned king of France.

•

1653 Oliver Cromwell assumed the title of Lord Protector of the Commonwealth of England, Scotland and Ireland.

•

1773 the Boston Tea Party took place.

•

1917 Arthur C Clarke, the science-fiction writer and futurist, was born in Minehead, Somerset.

•

1929 Britain's R100 airship had its first test flight.

•

1944 the Battle of the Bulge began in the Ardennes.

•

1969 MPs voted for the permanent abolition of the death penalty for murder.

•

1991 Kazakhstan declared independence from the Soviet Union.

17 DECEMBER

1538 King Henry VIII, who had declared himself head of the English Church, was excommunicated by Pope Paul III.

•

1843 Charles Dickens's *A Christmas Carol* was published, its first print run of 6,000 copies selling out by Christmas Day.

•

1903 the Wright brothers made the first powered flight at Kitty Hawk, North Carolina.

•

1983 an IRA bomb killed six people outside Harrods in London.

•

1986 Davina Thompson received the world's first heart, lung and liver transplant at Papworth Hospital, Cambridge.

•

1996 Sun Yaoting, the last surviving Chinese imperial eunuch, died aged 94.

18 DECEMBER

1839 in New York, John Draper made a daguerreotype of the moon, the first celestial photograph.

•

1849 the American astronomer William Bond took the first photograph of the moon through a telescope.

•

1865 slavery was officially abolished in the United States by the 13th Amendment.

•

1903 the US-Panama treaty placed the Canal Zone under American control.

•

1912 the discovery of the skull of a primitive hominid, known as the Piltdown Man, was announced; it was later found to be a hoax.

•

1987 Ivan Boesky, the Wall Street financier and insider trader, was jailed for three years.

19 DECEMBER

1154 Henry II was crowned King of England.

•

1783 William Pitt the Younger, 24, became the youngest British prime minister.

•

1863 in London, Frederick Walton patented his invention of linoleum.

•

1871 Samuel Clemens (the author Mark Twain) took out a patent for an improvement in adjustable and detachable garment straps: braces.

•

1956 Eastbourne doctor John Bodkin Adams was arrested on suspicion of murdering 160 patients; he was eventually acquitted of the charges.

•

1967 the prime minister of Australia, Harold Holt, was declared presumed dead after disappearing while swimming off Cheviot Beach, Victoria.

1560 the first general assembly of the Church of Scotland took place.

•

1848 Louis Napoleon Bonaparte was proclaimed president of France.

•

1880 Charles F Brush demonstrated his arc lamps along Broadway, preceding Edison's incandescent light bulb in commercial use.

•

1973 Spain's prime minister, Admiral Luis Carrero Blanco, was assassinated by a massive car bomb in Madrid.

•

1987 a collision between the Philippine ferry *Dona Paz* and a tanker caused the deaths of 4,386 passengers and crew, the worst peacetime tragedy at sea.

•

1999 after 400 years, Portugal returned Macau to Chinese rule.

•

2007 Queen Elizabeth II became the oldest sovereign of the United Kingdom, surpassing the age at death of Queen Victoria.

21 DECEMBER

1620 the Pilgrim Fathers landed in Plymouth, Massachusetts.

•

1799 the poet William Wordsworth, and his sister Dorothy, woke up for the first time in Dove Cottage, Grasmere, which would be his home until 1808 and the site of his greatest creativity.

•

1968 *Apollo 8*, which would become the first manned flight around the moon, was launched by a Saturn 5 booster from Cape Kennedy, Florida, US.

•

1988 a Pan American jumbo jet was blown up by a terrorist bomb and crashed on the Scottish border town of Lockerbie, killing 270 people.

1808 Beethoven's 5th and 6th Symphonies received their premieres in Vienna.

•

1849 the socialist activist (and future author of *Crime and Punishment*) Fyodor Dostoevsky received a last-minute reprieve from death by firing squad.

•

1882 Edward H Johnson, a colleague of Thomas Edison, created the first string of electric Christmas tree lights.

•

1894 falsely accused of supplying military secrets to the Germans, Alfred Dreyfus, a French army captain of Jewish descent, was convicted of treason.

•

1989 in the wake of the toppling of the Communist regime, Berlin's Brandenburg Gate reopened amidst scenes of joy.

23 DECEMBER

1787 HMS *Bounty*, commanded by William Bligh,
set sail for the South Seas.

1888 Van Gogh argued with Gauguin before cutting off
a piece of his own ear.

1920 the Government of Ireland Act was passed which five
months later saw the island divided into the six counties
of Northern Ireland, and the 26 of southern Ireland.

1972 an earthquake in Nicaragua killed 6,000 people,
injured 20,000 and left more than 250,000 homeless.

1986 *Voyager* landed in California, becoming the first
aircraft to fly non-stop around the world without refuelling.

24 DECEMBER

1818 in Arnsdorf, Austria, Franz Gruber, deputy organist of the Church of St Nicolas in Oberndorf, composed his one published work, the music for the poem *Silent Night* by the church's curate, Josef Mohr.

•

1828 the trial began of the grave-robber and murderer William Burke who, with William Hare, provided corpses for anatomists.

•

1903 the first English car registration plate, A1, was issued to Earl Russell, the brother of the philosopher Bertrand Russell.

•

1904 the largest theatre in London, the London Coliseum, now an opera house, opened as a variety theatre.

•

1979 Soviet troops invaded Afghanistan.

25 DECEMBER

597 St Augustine of Canterbury baptised 10,000 Anglo-Saxons in Kent.

•

1914 unofficial truces were organised between the combatants on the Western Front to mark Christmas.

•

1977 silent film star Charlie Chaplin died in Switzerland aged 88.

•

1989 following the Romanian Revolution, former dictator Nicolae Ceausescu and his wife Elena were executed by firing squad after a summary trial.

•

1991 Mikhail Gorbachev resigned as president of the Soviet Union, which was dissolved the following day.

•

2003 scientists attempted to contact the ill-fated probe *Beagle 2*, which had ceased transmissions shortly before landing on Mars.

26 DECEMBER

1898 Marie and Pierre Curie discovered radium while experimenting with a mineral form of uranium oxide.

•

1943 the German battlecruiser *Scharnhorst* was sunk in an engagement with British cruisers and the battleship HMS *Duke of York*.

•

1948 Bertrand Russell delivered the first in the BBC's series of Reith Lectures, his subject being Authority and the Individual.

•

1963 the Beatles released *I Want to Hold Your Hand* and *I Saw Her Standing There* in the US, marking the beginning of Beatlemania as an international phenomenon.

•

2004 more than 200,000 people died when tsunamis struck the Indian Ocean.

27 DECEMBER

537 the Roman emperor Justinian attended the consecration of the church of St Sophia (later to become a mosque) in Constantinople.

•

1831 Charles Darwin left England for South America, beginning his near five-year voyage aboard HMS *Beagle*.

•

1836 the deadliest avalanche in British history occurred when banked snow fell from cliffs above Lewes, Sussex, and killed eight people.

•

1904 the first performance of JM Barrie's *Peter Pan* took place in London.

•

1923 Japan's prince regent, Hirohito, survived an assassination attempt.

•

1977 *Star Wars* was released in Britain.

•

2016 *Star Wars* actress Carrie Fisher died aged 60.

28 DECEMBER

1065 Westminster Abbey was consecrated.

•

1879 the Tay Bridge, Dundee, collapsed as a train crossed it, killing 78 people.

1895 the Lumière brothers projected the first moving pictures onto the wall of the Grand Café on the Boulevard des Capucines, Paris.

•

1904 the first weather reports relayed by wireless telegraphy were published in London.

•

1912 the first streetcars began carrying passengers in San Francisco.

•

1918 the December 14 general election results were declared, after the votes of soldiers serving overseas had been counted. Countess Markievicz took the Dublin St Patrick's constituency, making her the first woman elected to the House of Commons. As a member of Sinn Fein, the countess never took up her seat.

•

1950 the Peak District was designated Britain's first national park.

•

2016 the actress Debbie Reynolds (*Singin' in the Rain*), and mother of Carrie Fisher, died aged 84.

1170 Thomas Becket was murdered in Canterbury cathedral by four knights loyal to King Henry II.

1930 Radio Luxembourg began broadcasting.

1937 the Irish Free State changed its name to Eire as the new constitution was implemented.

1951 the first transistorised hearing aid went on sale in America.

1952 a coelacanth caught in the Mozambique Channel became only the second of its species to be identified in modern times.

1975 the Sex Discrimination and Equal Pay Acts came into force in Britain.

1998 six people died when huge seas struck yachts racing from Sydney to Hobart.

1672 the King's band of 24 violins, formed by
King Charles II and led by John Banister, held
the earliest documented public concert in Britain.

•

1887 the home secretary received a petition addressed
to Queen Victoria, appealing for public houses to be closed
on Sundays and signed by more than a million women.

•

1894 Amelia Bloomer, pioneer of practical clothing
for women, died in Iowa aged 72.

•

1916 a group of Russian noblemen led by Prince Youssoupoff
murdered Rasputin.

•

1922 Russia officially became the Union of Soviet Socialist
Republics (USSR).

1695 the window tax was imposed, levied according
to how many windows a house possessed.

•

1759 in Dublin, Arthur Guinness began his
brewing operations.

•

1923 the BBC first broadcast the chimes of Big Ben
to announce the new year.

•

1938 Dr RN Harger's drunkometer, the first breathalyser
for motorists, was introduced in Indianapolis, Indiana.

•

1960 the farthing ceased to be legal tender in Britain.

•

1973 during an energy crisis, Edward Heath's government
introduced a three-day week for industry.

•

1999 Boris Yeltsin resigned as president of Russia,
and was succeeded by Vladimir Putin.

DATE INDEX